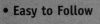

Internet Explorer
Made Simple

Sam Kennington

MADE SIMPLE
BOOKS

Made Simple
An imprint of Butterworth-Heinemann
Linacre House, Jordan Hill, Oxford OX2 8DP
A division of Reed Educational and Professional Publishing Ltd

℞ A member of the Reed Elsevier plc group

OXFORD BOSTON JOHANNESBURG
MELBOURNE NEW DELHI SINGAPORE

First published 1997
Reprinted 1997

© Sam Kennington 1997

TRADEMARKS/REGISTERED TRADEMARKS
Computer hardware and software brand names mentioned in this book are protected
by their respective trademarks and are acknowledged.

British Library Cataloguing in Publication Data
A catalogue record for this book is available from the British Library

ISBN 0 7506 3513 4

Typeset by P.K.McBride, Southampton

Archtype, Bash Casual, Cotswold and Gravity fonts from Advanced Graphics Ltd
Icons designed by Sarah Ward © 1994
Printed and bound in Great Britain by Scotprint, Musselburgh, Scotland

Contents

Preface

Since first appearing two years ago, Microsoft's Internet Explorer has been refined and expanded. Its current version (3.0), provides an excellent set of tools for working on the Internet.

Internet Explorer has:

- An excellent browser for surfing the World Wide Web. It's fast, responsive and easy to control.

- A Mail window for sending and receiving e-mail messages. And if you want to send a file to a friend, it can be simply attached to a message – and detached at the other end.

- A News window for accessing the many thousands of newsgroups, through which enthusiasts from around the world share their interests.

And if you want to create your own Web pages, Internet Assistant can be linked to Word (or to any of the other Office applications).

This book will show you how to set up Internet Explorer to suit your ways of working; start you off on your explorations of the Web; explain how to send and receive messages, articles and files through the Mail and News systems; and give an introduction to creating your own Web pages with HTML.

Take note

Unlike other leading browsers, Interent Explorer is not shareware – it is freeware!

1 Setting up

Downloading

If you do not yet have Internet Explorer 3.0, you can pick it up – free – wherever you see the button.

There are versions for most operating systems and for many languages. You can also choose between a minimum, typical or full installation – unless you are really keen to save disk space and/or connection time, go for the full installation.

(1) Go to Microsoft's Download Area

1 Start from an *Explorer* button, or go to **www.microsoft.com** and select **Products**, then **free download** then **Internet Explorer**.

2 Select the latest version for your **system**.

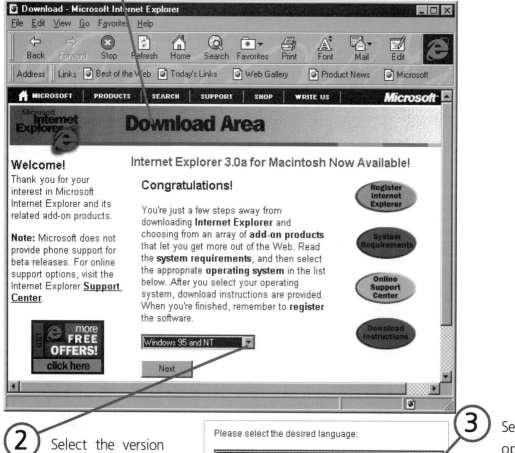

(2) Select the version

Click **Next** after each stage

(3) Set the other options

3 Select the **Language** and **Install size**.

4 Select a site close to you. As the data will go through fewer links to reach you, it should travel faster.

5 At the virus warning, select **Save it to disk** – store the file in a temporary folder.

Save it to disk

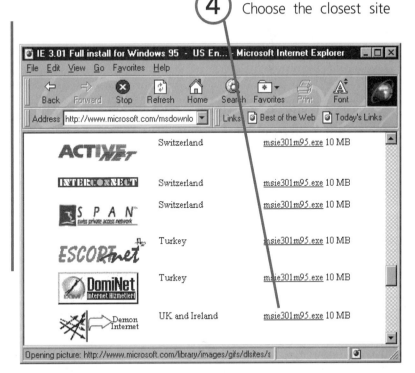

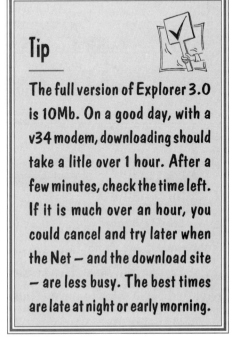

Choose the closest site

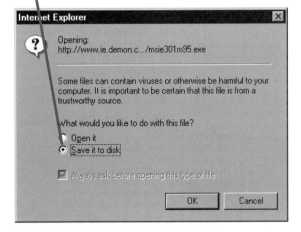

You get this warning when Explorer meets certain types of files. If desired, it can be turned off for selected types. (See page 74 for more on downloading.)

Tip

The full version of Explorer 3.0 is 10Mb. On a good day, with a v34 modem, downloading should take a litle over 1 hour. After a few minutes, check the time left. If it is much over an hour, you could cancel and try later when the Net – and the download site – are less busy. The best times are late at night or early morning.

Installation

Internet Explorer is distributed as a self-extracting Zip file with a built-in setup routine. This reduces installation almost to a single click.

(1) Close down everything except My Computer or Explorer

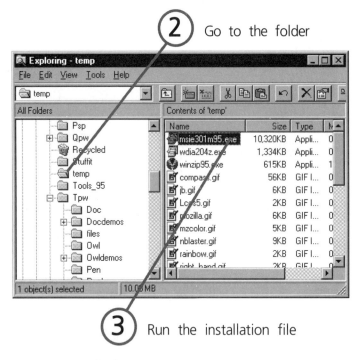

(2) Go to the folder

(3) Run the installation file

Basic steps

1 Close down all applications except **My Computer** or **Explorer**.

2 Go to your temporary folder.

3 Find the file – its name will begin **msie30...** and double-click to run the **Setup** program.

4 If you do not want the Mail or News, click **Yes** to select the optional components.

5 Tick the Mail and/or News as required.

6 In Windows 95 you should find that Explorer has been added to the **Start** menu and the Desktop.

Take note

The Mail (Chapter 7) and News (Chapter 8) facilities are optional. If you do not intend to use them, save some space and don't install them. If necessary, you can run the Setup routine again later to install them – it will not affect the existing Explorer files.

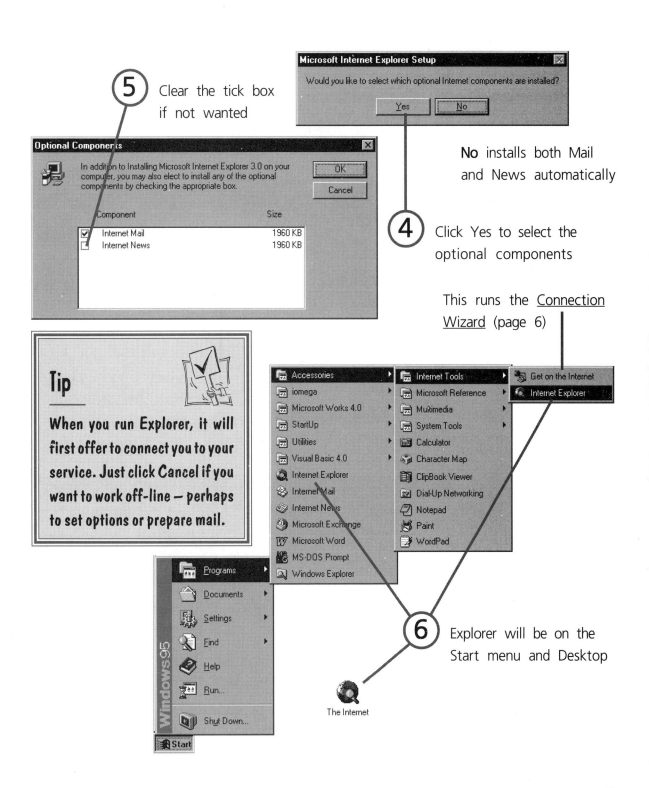

⑤ Clear the tick box
if not wanted

Microsoft Internet Explorer Setup

Would you like to select which optional Internet components are installed?

[Yes]   [No]

No installs both Mail
and News automatically

Optional Components

In addition to Installing Microsoft Internet Explorer 3.0 on your
computer, you may also elect to install any of the optional
components by checking the appropriate box.

[OK]
[Cancel]

Component	Size
☑ Internet Mail	1960 KB
☐ Internet News	1960 KB

④ Click Yes to select the
optional components

This runs the <u>Connection
Wizard</u> (page 6)

Tip

When you run Explorer, it will
first offer to connect you to your
service. Just click Cancel if you
want to work off-line – perhaps
to set options or prepare mail.

Accessories ▶	Internet Tools ▶	🔧 Get on the Internet
iomega ▶	Microsoft Reference ▶	Internet Explorer
Microsoft Works 4.0 ▶	Multimedia ▶	
StartUp ▶	System Tools ▶	
Utilities ▶	Calculator	
Visual Basic 4.0 ▶	Character Map	
Internet Explorer	ClipBook Viewer	
Internet Mail	Dial-Up Networking	
Internet News	Notepad	
Microsoft Exchange	Paint	
Microsoft Word	WordPad	
MS-DOS Prompt		
Windows Explorer		

Programs ▶
Documents ▶
Settings ▶
Find ▶
Help
Run...
Shut Down...

Windows 95

🅰 Start

⑥ Explorer will be on the
Start menu and Desktop

The Internet

5

Making the connection

Before you can get on-line, you must tell Explorer about your service provider. The Connection Wizard makes this simple – but you must have the necessary information to hand at the start. You need to know:

● your provider's phone number

● your provider's DNS Server Addresses – they will be in the form of four sets of digits, like this: 190.99.134.29

● you provider's Mail and News servers' names – probably something like '*mail.myprovider.co.uk*'

● your IP address – or not! Many systems allocate a new address when you log on

● your user name, e-mail address and password

1 Click on **Start**, point to **Programs**, then **Accessories**, **Internet Tools** and select **Get on the Internet**.

2 At the **Setup Options**, select *Current* if you already have a connection; *Automatic* if you need to find a service provider; or *Manual* otherwise.

3 Continue through the Wizard, responding to prompts and clicking **Next** after each stage. Watch for the panels illustrated opposite.

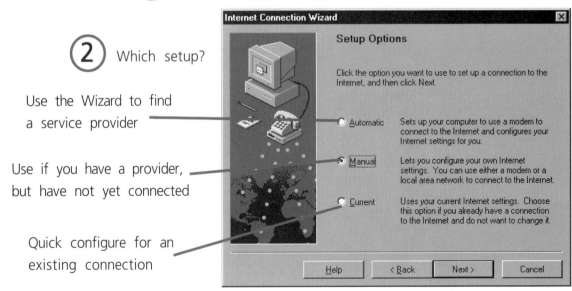

| Accessories | Internet Tools | Get on the Internet |
| | | Internet Explorer |

(1) Get on the Internet!

(2) Which setup?

Use the Wizard to find a service provider

Use if you have a provider, but have not yet connected

Quick configure for an existing connection

Internet Connection Wizard

Setup Options

Click the option you want to use to set up a connection to the Internet, and then click Next.

○ Automatic — Sets up your computer to use a modem to connect to the Internet and configures your Internet settings for you.

● Manual — Lets you configure your own Internet settings. You can use either a modem or a local area network to connect to the Internet.

○ Current — Uses your current Internet settings. Choose this option if you already have a connection to the Internet and do not want to change it.

Help | < Back | Next > | Cancel

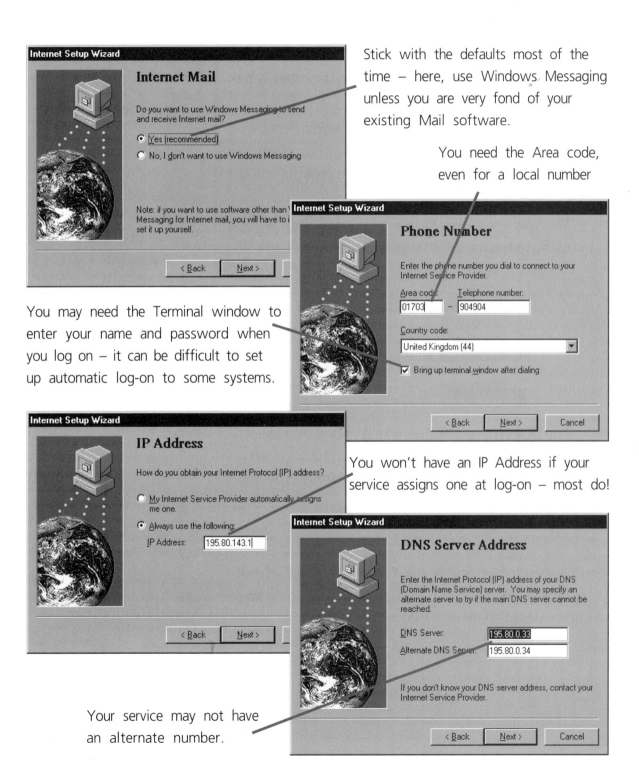

Internet Mail

Do you want to use Windows Messaging to send and receive Internet mail?

○ Yes (recommended)
○ No, I don't want to use Windows Messaging

Note: if you want to use software other than Messaging for Internet mail, you will have to set it up yourself.

< Back   Next >

Stick with the defaults most of the time – here, use Windows Messaging unless you are very fond of your existing Mail software.

You need the Area code, even for a local number

Phone Number

Enter the phone number you dial to connect to your Internet Service Provider.

Area code: Telephone number:
01703   –   904904

Country code:
United Kingdom (44)

☑ Bring up terminal window after dialing

< Back   Next >   Cancel

You may need the Terminal window to enter your name and password when you log on – it can be difficult to set up automatic log-on to some systems.

IP Address

How do you obtain your Internet Protocol (IP) address?

○ My Internet Service Provider automatically assigns me one.
○ Always use the following:
    IP Address: 195.80.143.1

< Back   Next >

You won't have an IP Address if your service assigns one at log-on – most do!

DNS Server Address

Enter the Internet Protocol (IP) address of your DNS (Domain Name Service) server. You may specify an alternate server to try if the main DNS server cannot be reached.

DNS Server: 195.80.0.33
Alternate DNS Server: 195.80.0.34

If you don't know your DNS server address, contact your Internet Service Provider.

< Back   Next >   Cancel

Your service may not have an alternate number.

The browser window

The Toolbar

Internet Explorer has several windows, but the one that you start in – and the one you will almost certainly use most – is the browser window.

The main part of the window is used for the display of Web pages. Above this are the control elements. The **Menu bar** is always present. The commonly used commands are duplicated in the **Toolbar buttons**.

- The **Address** shows you where you are. You can type a URL (page 26) here to open a location (page 30). The last 10 URLs that you typed are stored here, for ease of revisiting.

- The **Links** (page 13) offer an easy way to connect to selected places. Initially, they connect to pages on Microsoft's site. These are also on the Microsoft on the Web menu (Chapter 3.)

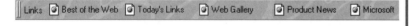

The Toolbar display is optional. You can turn off the whole thing from the View menu, or fine tune its appearance using the General Options (page 10).

Back — Previous page

Forward — Next page (if loaded)

Stop — Stop loading

Refresh — Reload current page

Home — Go to your Start page (page 13)

Search — Go to Microsoft's Search (page 45)

Favorites — Open Favorites menu (page 64)

Print — Print the current page

Font — Change Font size

Mail — Mail (chapter 7) and News (chapter 8)

Take note

If you install Internet Assistant, you will also have this button. Edit

Basic steps

- ❏ **Display options**
- **1** Click on **View**.
- **2** Click on **Toolbar** or **Status Bar** to turn its display on (✓) or off.

① Open View

② Click to turn on or off

View
- ✓ Toolbar
- ✓ Status Bar
- Fonts ▶
- Stop   Esc
- Refresh   F5
- Source
- Options...

Tip

For better control of the display, use the View – Options... (page 10).

Title of current page

Links buttons

Menu bar

Toolbar buttons

Address

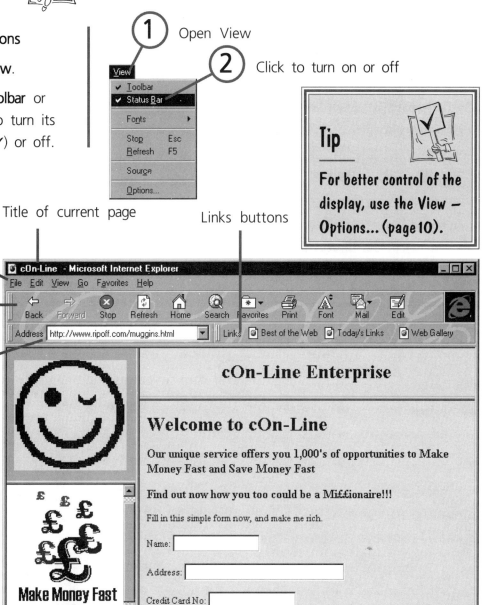

Status bar – shows progress of incoming page

9

General options

You can control many aspects of Explorer's display, and of how it works. All aspects are controlled through the various Options panels.

The General options define the appearance of the toolbar and the display area.

Pictures, audio and video files on Web pages are sometimes essential, often merely decorative and always slow to download. Turn them off for faster browsing – you can turn these back on and reload a page to view the files, or click on a non-displayed image to load it for viewing.

Basic steps

1 Open the **View** menu and select **Options**...

2 Open the **General** panel.

3 Click the tick boxes to turn options on or off.

4 Click **Apply** to test the effect of a setting.

5 Go to the next panel.

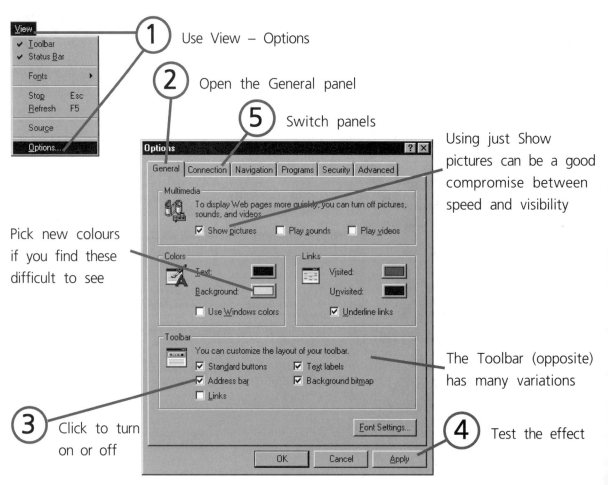

Use View – Options

Open the General panel

Switch panels

Using just Show pictures can be a good compromise between speed and visibility

Pick new colours if you find these difficult to see

The Toolbar (opposite) has many variations

Click to turn on or off

Test the effect

Tailor-made toolbars

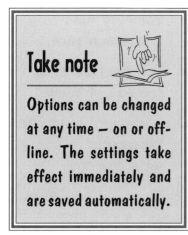
The aim here is to strike the balance between ease of use and the size of the page viewing area. These options may be best set after you have been using Explorer for a while.

● Each part of the toolbar can be turned on or off.

● Bars can be dragged up or down around the area – squeeze two onto one line to save space, or set them one above the other.

● Where bars share a line, you can move the dividing line between them, or expand one to full width.

Default

All bars visible
Buttons with text

Click here to toggle between current width and full width

Drag to adjust the split

Maximum

Each bar on
a new line

Point here, hold the left button down and drag up or down

Minimum

Toolbar buttons
only – without text

You can even turn off the buttons, and work from the menu commands only.

Connection options

Running the Connection Wizard (page 6) will have filled in the essential information on this panel, but there are a couple of options that need your attention.

● If Connect as needed... is turned on, Explorer will call up the Connect dialog box if you click a link while using the software off-line. This can be useful.

● Turn on the automatic disconnect if there is any possibility of you leaving the machine unattended and running up phone bills. But don't set too short a time or it will cut you off while you are reading a long page!

1 Switch to the **Connection** panel.

2 Tick the **Connect as needed...** if wanted.

3 If you want to use the **Disconnect...** tick it and set a time limit.

4 Go to the next panel.

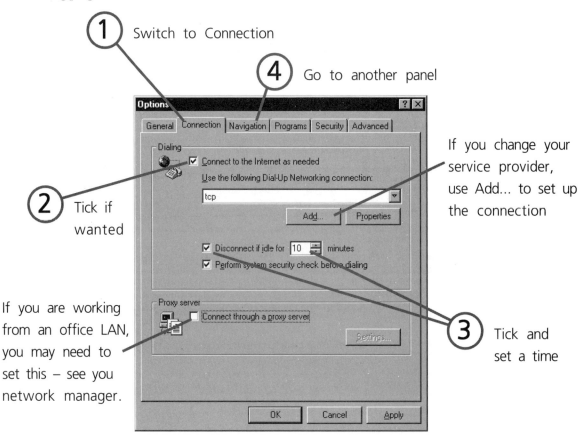

① Switch to Connection

④ Go to another panel

② Tick if wanted

If you change your service provider, use Add... to set up the connection

If you are working from an office LAN, you may need to set this – see you network manager.

③ Tick and set a time

Basic steps

Navigation

❑ **Reassigning links**

1 Go on-line and find a page that you would like to use as a **Start** or **Search** page, or create a quick **Link** to.

2 Switch to the **Navigation** panel.

3 Open the **Page** list.

4 Select a link.

5 Click **Use Current**.

With the default settings, Explorer connects to Microsoft's site on start-up, and has links to various other Microsoft pages in its Search and Links buttons. These can all be reassigned through the Navigation panel.

The History Folder (page 32) is also controlled from here. This stores the text and images of visited pages, allowing you to revisit them off-line. The longer you keep them, the more disk space it consumes.

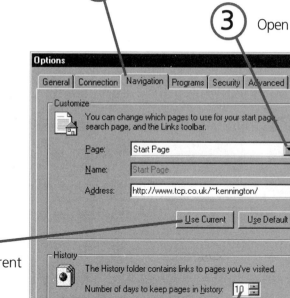

② Switch to Navigation

③ Open the Page list

④ Pick a link

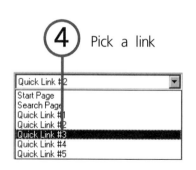

⑤ Click Use Current

Take note

You can only reassign a link to a new page while you are on-line and connected to that page.

If you do not look back at old pages much, cut this right down and save disk space.

File types and viewers

Much of the material that is on the Web can be viewed directly through Explorer – the built-in routines can handle audio files and graphics in the commonly-used formats.

You will also find other types of files on the Web, such as TIF and BMP graphics, Word documents and PostScript files. If you have programs that can handle these, and have already registered the file types, Internet Explorer will run the programs when it meets the files.

As you surf the Net, you will meet new file types – and if you hunt through the <u>shareware sites</u> (page 76) you can find the programs to view them. After you have installed a new viewer, link its file type through the Programs panel. The procedure is much the same as in Windows 95 Explorer.

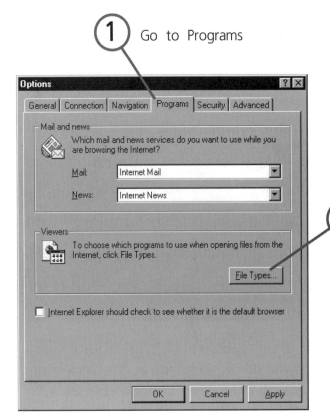

① Go to Programs

② Click File Types ...

1 Go to the **Programs** panel.

2 Click **File Types**...

3 At the **File Types** dialog box, click **New Type**...

4 Enter a **Description** and the **.Extension** for that type – include the dot!

5 Click **New**.

6 At the **New Action** dialog, type **open**. Another *New Action* you might add is **print**.

7 Click **Browse** and locate the program.

8 If you turn on **Confirm Open After Download**, you will be get a Save or View? choice when you download a file.

Tip

You can find suitable viewers for almost all types of files on the Web.

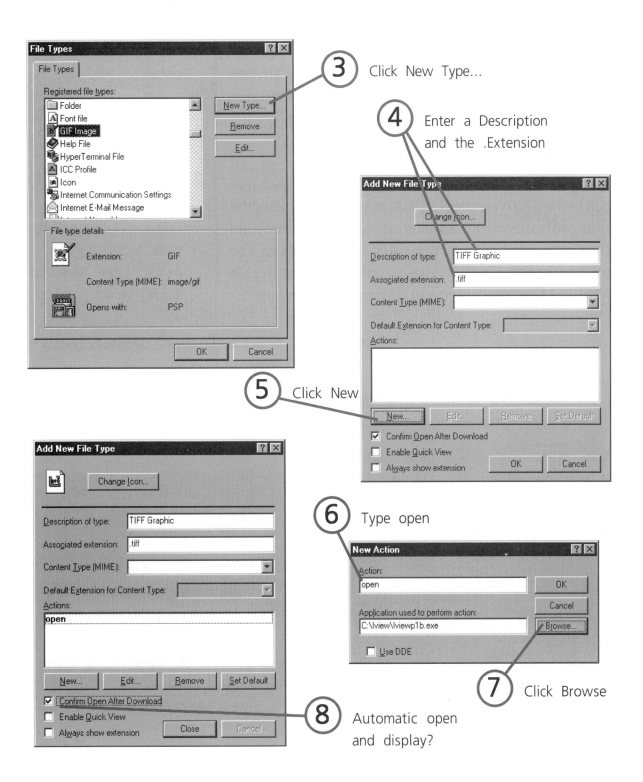

File Types

File Types

Registered file types:
- Folder
- Font file
- GIF Image
- Help File
- HyperTerminal File
- ICC Profile
- Icon
- Internet Communication Settings
- Internet E-Mail Message

New Type...
Remove
Edit...

File type details

Extension: GIF

Content Type (MIME):   image/gif

Opens with: PSP

OK   Cancel

③ Click New Type...

④ Enter a Description and the .Extension

Add New File Type

Change Icon...

Description of type: TIFF Graphic
Associated extension: .tiff
Content Type (MIME):
Default Extension for Content Type:
Actions:

New...   Edit...   Remove   Set Default

☑ Confirm Open After Download
☐ Enable Quick View
☐ Always show extension

OK   Cancel

⑤ Click New

Add New File Type

Change Icon...

Description of type: TIFF Graphic
Associated extension: .tiff
Content Type (MIME):
Default Extension for Content Type:
Actions:
open

New...   Edit...   Remove   Set Default

☑ Confirm Open After Download
☐ Enable Quick View
☐ Always show extension

Close   Cancel

⑥ Type open

New Action

Action:
open

Application used to perform action:
C:\lview\lviewp1b.exe

☐ Use DDE

OK
Cancel
Browse...

⑦ Click Browse

⑧ Automatic open and display?

15

Security

There are several distinct aspects to security in Explorer. The first is about protecting younger users – or anyone else who might be offended – from the unacceptable material that lurks in various corners of the Net.

Content Advisor

This allows you to control the levels of sex'n'violence that can be viewed over the Net. It does this by checking the ratings of a site when it is visited. If the ratings are beyond the limits you have set, access is denied. This can be overridden by the use of the password, should you decide a site has been overrated and is suitable for viewing.

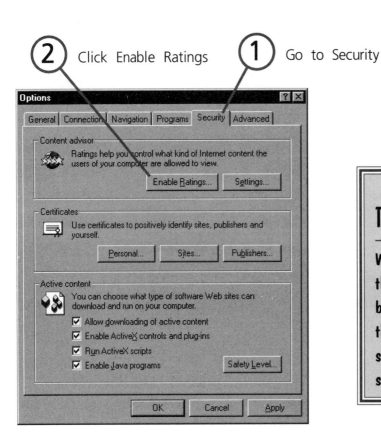

② Click Enable Ratings ① Go to Security

Basic steps

1 Go to the **Security** panel.

2 Click **Enable Ratings**.

3 Decide on a **Password** and enter it – twice.

4 On the **Ratings** panel, set the limit for each Category – moving the slider to the right permits higher levels of sex'n'violence.

5 On the **General** panel you can allow people to see unrated sites, or allow others to use your password to view restricted sites.

Tip

With Content Advisor enabled, the Net is a safer place for kids, but for even greater control over their activities on the Net, you should use SurfWatch or other safety software.

3 Set the password

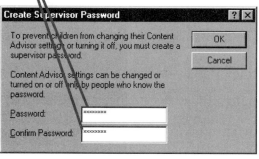

The Ratings are set by the (RSAC) Recreational Standards Advisory Council. At the time of writing over 15,000 sites had been rated.

Click here while on-line to find out about the RSAC

4 Decide your limits

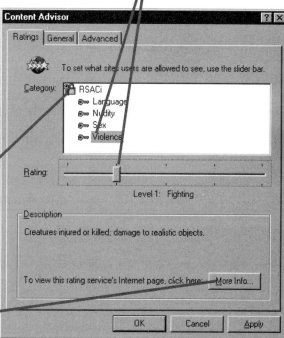

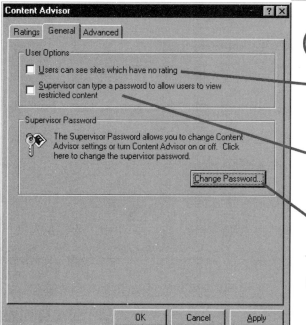

5 Set the General options

An unrated site is not necessarily unsuitable – but is more likely to be

Turn this on to allow you – or any authorised person – to override a restriction

The password can – and should be – changed regularly

Certificates

These are issued by some sites, and ensure that any traffic between you and the site is not diverted at either end. Some sites issue personal certificates to identify you when you are dealing with them.

For most of the time, these can be left alone – the system is secure – but a little housekeeping is needed occasionally. Each certificate has an expiration date. Once it is expired, it should be removed to keep the system tidy.

Basic steps

❑ **Checking certificates**

1 Go to the **Security** panel.

2 Click **Sites**....

3 Select each certificate in turn and click **View Certificate**.

4 Check the **Expiration date**, and if it is passed, **Delete** the certificate.

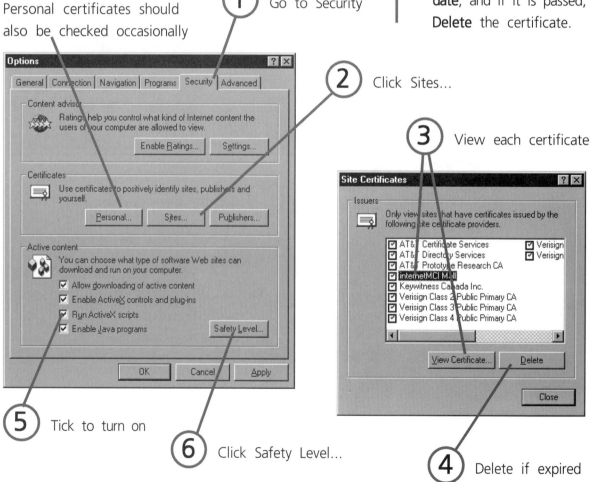

Personal certificates should also be checked occasionally

1 Go to Security

2 Click Sites...

3 View each certificate

5 Tick to turn on

6 Click Safety Level...

4 Delete if expired

Basic steps

❏ Controlling content

5 Turn the **Active content** *on* for better browsing, *off* for higher security.

6 Click **Safety Level....**

7 Set the level to **High**.

8 Click **OK**.

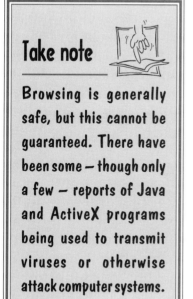

Take note

Browsing is generally safe, but this cannot be guaranteed. There have been some – though only a few – reports of Java and ActiveX programs being used to transmit viruses or otherwise attack computer systems.

Active content

An increasing number of Web pages have embedded within them multimedia files and applets (small applications) written in Java or ActiveX – programming languages written for Internet use. These should not be able to mess with your hard disks or access your data (and Java is more secure than ActiveX in that respect), but hackers love a challenge...

Active content makes browsing more interesting, and if you stick to Certified sites, should create no problems. But just to be on the safe side, set your Safety Level to High, and let Explorer watch out for potential dangers.

⑦ Select High security

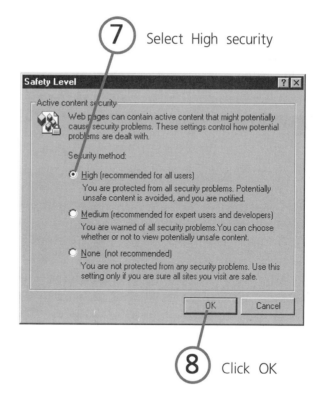

⑧ Click OK

Advanced options

Basic steps

Don't be put off by the name – there are some pretty basic options here as well!

Warnings

If the warnings are on, you will get a message when data is about to be sent from your system, or be written onto your disks. At that point, you can stop the transfer if you like. In general, it is good to have a chance to assess the security risk before a transfer, but you can overdo this.

● When sending, it is a nuisance to have to clear the warning before submitting every (one-line) Search query (page 45), but useful before submitting a form.

● Cookies are sent by sites to log your visit – a kind of registration. As you can't visit if you don't accept the cookies, you may as well switch off these warnings.

❑ **Warnings**

1 Go to the **Advanced** panel.

2 Turn on the **send** Warning for *more than one line*.

3 Turn off the **cookie** warning, unless you are very concerned about security.

❑ **Temporary files**

4 Click **Settings...**

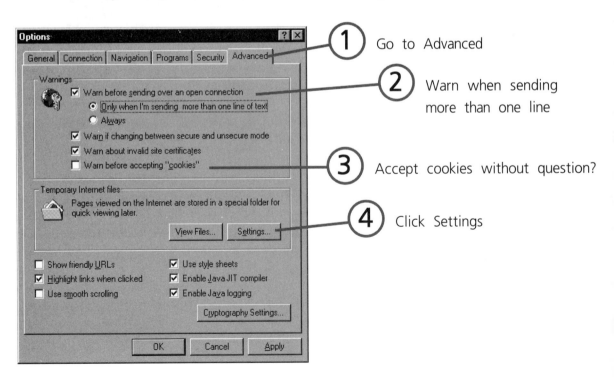

(1) Go to Advanced

(2) Warn when sending more than one line

(3) Accept cookies without question?

(4) Click Settings

Temporary Internet files

5 Set it to check Every time you start – there is no point in checking again if you revisit a page during one session.

6 Pull the slider to allocate storage space. 1% of a 1Gb drive is 10Mb – enough for dozens of pages.

When you visit a page, Explorer stores its text and images in its temporary file space. When you then revisit that page, Explorer first checks the store, and if it finds an up-to-date copy of the page will load from there rather than over the Internet. A large storage area can speed up your surfing if you regularly revisit the same sites – and their pages don't change too often. If you rarely go back to a site, the storage area can be kept small.

5 Once a session is enough

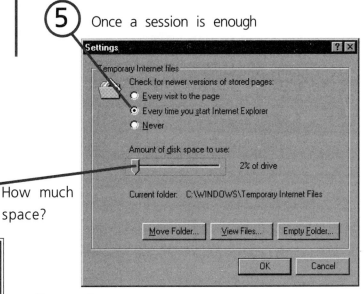

6 How much space?

Other options

The left-hand column options affect the screen display – play with these!

● The Java JIT (Just In Time) compiler automatically compiles and runs a Java applet when Explorer downloads it from a page.

● The Java logger keeps track of anything that a Java applet does to your system. Enable this if you enable the JIT compiler.

Summary

❑ Explorer is available in versions for most types of computer and operating systems.

❑ The software can be downloaded from Microsoft's home page, or wherever you see an **Internet Explorer** button.

❑ Explorer is largely **self-installing** and does some of the necessary configuration for you.

❑ The **Toolbar**, **Address** and **Links buttons** can be moved or removed, to create a larger viewing area.

❑ To get it working just the way you want it, spend some time on the **options panels**.

❑ When setting the **Connection** options, you will need addresses and other details from your service provider.

❑ You can use the **Links** buttons to create quick links to any site on the Internet.

❑ Explorer can handle most types of files that you meet on the Web, and will launch other applications in your system to handle **registered file types**.

❑ The **Security** options help to keep your system safe from on-line dangers, and to restrict the sites that can be reached by other users of your system.

2 Browsing the Web

Net-speak

Access provider
An organisation that gives businesses and individuals access to the Internet. Sometimes called *service providers*.

Applet
A small Java application, embedded in a Web page. Commonly used to create flashy titles or scroll messages in the status bar.

Browse
Move from one place to another on the Web, stopping to pick up interesting bits as you go.

Catalog
An organised list of Web sites and other Internet resources. The best catalogs offer comprehensive coverage of what's on the Net, with summaries of what you will find at different places. Also known as Directories. (Chapter 4.)

Directory
See Catalog.

Download
Copy a file from somewhere on the Net, into your system.

FTP
File Transfer Protocol. The standard way of copying files over the Net. Servers that hold databases of shareware, freeware and other files are known as <u>FTP sites</u> (page 78).

Home page
The top level page of a set of related pages.

Host
A computer providing some kind of service, such as holding files for users to download.

HTTP
(HyperText Transfer Protocol) The way that Web pages are linked together. Browsers can read HTTP links and use them to find Web pages. (See page 26.)

Take note

This list of jargon covers only the barest essentials — just enough so that you do not get too confused on your first journeys into Cyberspace.

If you want to learn to speak like a real nettie, surf over to:

http://www.netlingo.com

Java	A programming language mainly used to create applets for Web pages, though it can also produce stand-alone programs.
JavaScript	Based on Java, but much simplified. Its commands are written into Web pages and executed when the page is opened.
Newbie	Newcomer to the Net. When you come across disparaging references to newbies, remember that everyone was a newbie once.
Page	A combination of text, graphics, sound and other files that produce a screen display.
Search engine	A system that maintains a database or index of information, pages and/or files on the Internet, and offers users a means of searching through it (chapter 3).
Server	A computer providing a service to Internet users. Your access provider will have a mail server to act as a 'post office' for your <u>mail</u> (chapter 7), and a news server to hold the articles from <u>the newsgroups</u> (chapter 8).
Shareware	Software that can be downloaded free, for trial use, with the request that you pay (a small fee) if you continue to use it.
Site	An organisation's place on the Internet, holding one or more linked pages.
Surf	Move around the Web – and other parts of the Internet – to see what's happening.
URL	Uniform Resource Locator – the address of something on the Internet (page 26).

URLs and hypertext

Uniform Resource Locators

Every page on the Web, every file in an FTP site (page 78), every news group (page 106) and every e-mail user (page 90) has a Uniform Resource Locator. These tell where and *how* to get to the item.

World Wide Web page URLs look like this:

http://www.heinemann.co.uk/bh/simple/simple.html

http: (**h**ypertext **t**ransfer **p**rotocol) this is a Web page.

www.heinemann.co.uk – the domain, or address of an organisation

bh/simple – the path to the directory

simple.html – the name of the file that creates the page.

Other URLS that you may meet are:

ftp: (**f**ile **t**ransfer **p**rotocol) – a file that can be downloaded from the archives of an FTP site (page 78).

news: the name of a newsgroup – linking to this will access the current set of articles in that group.

mailto: an e-mail address – simplifies sending e-mail to the linked user.

Hypertext

The World Wide Web is based on hypertext links. These are URLs embedded in the text or images of Web pages. Clicking on such a link makes Explorer try to connect to the identified item. Depending on the nature of the URL, Explorer will jump to a Web page, start to download a file, bring in news articles or open the Mail window (page 86) so that you can write to the person.

Take note

Web URLs don't always include a page name. It is often missed out for the home page of a site or the top level of a set of pages in a directory.

Punctuation is crucial. The slashes that separate the parts of the URL are forward slashes – not the backslashes that are used in DOS and Windows.

Personal home pages often have a tilde (~) before the user's name. e.g.

www.inet.co.uk/~jobloggs

Hypertext links

Pointing to hypertext linked images or words, makes the cursor change to a hand and the URL appear in the status bar at the bottom of the window.

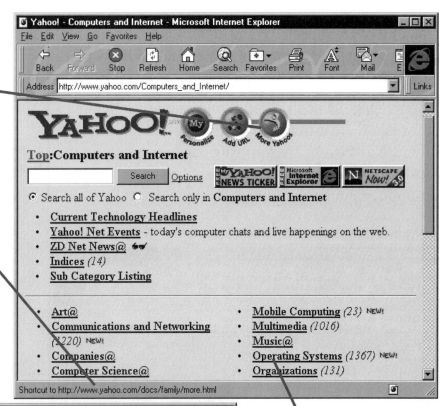

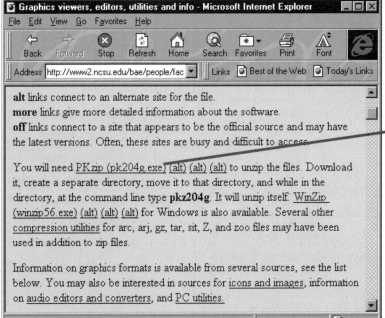

Hypertext links may be listed in a menu or embedded in the text.

They are normally shown underlined and in blue.

If the place has been visited recently, its link will be shown in a different colour – normally magenta.

Image maps

Image maps are a special type of hypertext linked graphic. These can have any number of links embedded into them, each in its own area of the image.

In some image maps, like the Internet Resources Metamap shown below, it is quite clear what each part links to. In others, like those on the opposite page, you may have to look carefully at the picture – or perhaps just click away until you hit something!

Tip

If you want to include an image map in your own home page, you can easily create one using MapEdit – find it at:

http://www.boutell.com

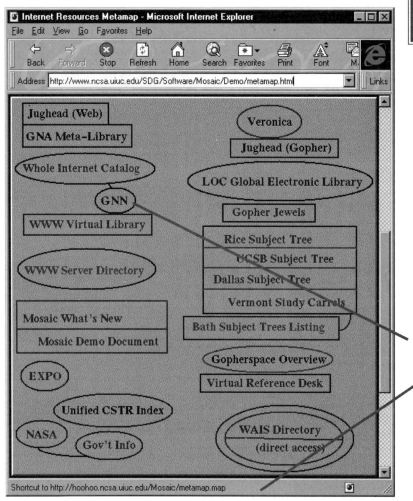

With image maps, the status bar does not show the URL when you are point to a link. All it shows are the coordinates of the cursor position.

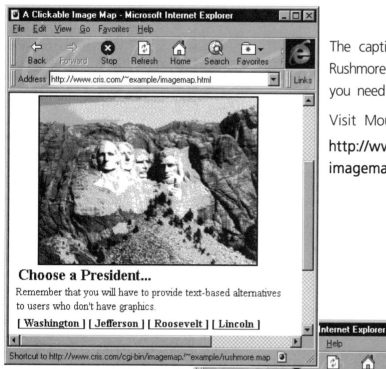

The caption to this image of Mount Rushmore should give you a clue — if you need one — as to where to click.

Visit Mount Rushmore at:

http://www.cris.com/~example/imagemap.html

This ray traced image looks even better in colour. It is not actually very helpful as an image map, but is not really meant to be. This is a fun demo from NCSA's HTTP development team. FInd it at:

http://hoohoo.ncsa.uiuc.edu/docs/info/Scripts.html

Opening locations

Clicking on hypertext links is the simplest way to browse the Web, but you have to find some links in the first place, and sometimes will have come across an interesting URL but don't have a ready-made link to it. No problem!

You can go to any place on the Internet as long as you have its URL. Actually, that is not quite true. You will occasionally come across the URLs of pages or files that can only be accessed by authorised people. Within a company or educational site, for example, some places may be open to the public, others restricted to members of the organisation.

Basic steps

1 If you have included the **Address** slot in your toolbar, type the URL directly into it.

Otherwise:

2 Open the **File** menu and select **Open**.

3 Type the URL into the **Open** dialog box.

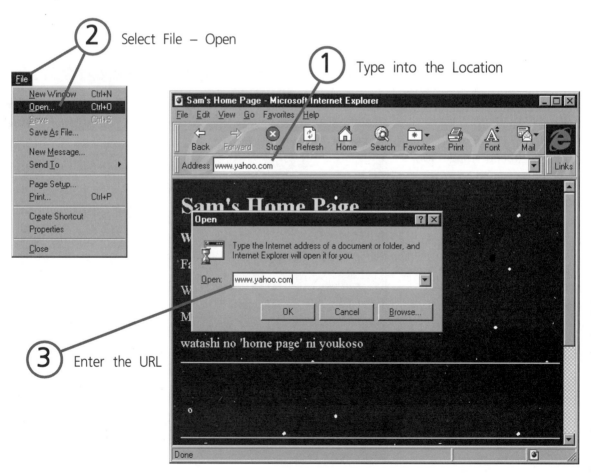

② Select File – Open

① Type into the Location

③ Enter the URL

Basic steps

...and re-opening them

❑ **Re-using addresses**

1 Drop down the **Address** list.

2 Click on a URL.

❑ **Returning to a page**

3 Click **Back**, or use **Go – Back** to return to the previous page.

4 Open the **Go** menu and select a title to visit a page from earlier in the same session.

Once you have been to a place, you have several simple ways back to it. Here are three:

● The **Back** and **Forward** buttons will move you through pages you have visited during the session.

● The **Go** menu lists the last five pages that you visited during the session.

● The **Address** drop-down list contains the URLs that you typed in. These are saved between sessions.

Drop down the list

Back one page

Select an address

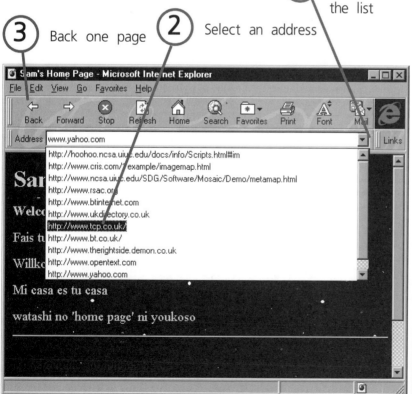

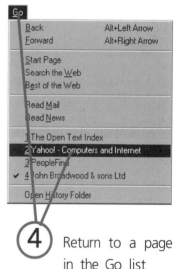

Return to a page in the Go list

Take note

The Forward button becomes active after you have gone Back.

The History Folder

As you browse, each page you visit is recorded in the History Folder. It is stored as an Internet Shortcut – i.e. a URL link – giving you a quick way to get back to any of those places. The files that make up the page are stored in the Temporary Internet Files folder. They can also be accessed directly from there.

1 Open the **Go** menu and select **Open History Folder**.

2 Double-click on the page's title.

3 If you are on-line, Explorer will connect to the page.

If you are off-line, the page will be pulled up from the Temporary Internet Files store.

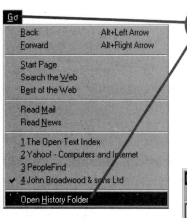

Use Go – Open History Folder

Double-click on the page

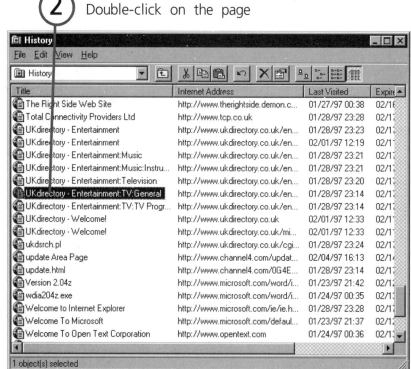

Unwanted items can be deleted – right click for the short menu and select Delete

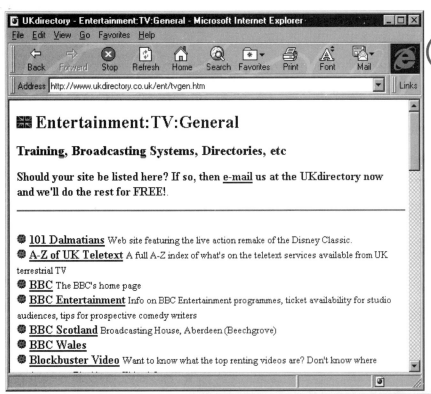

③ The page will be called up – either over the Net, or from the store

Tip

You can re-open pages from the Temporary Internet Files folder. You can also view the embedded images from here, though identifying them can be tricky.

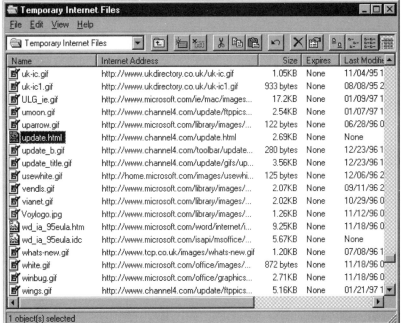

33

Saving pages

The Temporary Internet Files folder is just that – temporary! When you come across a page that you want for long-term reference you can save it as a file on your hard disk. It can then be opened from there at any time later.

Saved files should be easy to locate – you named them and stored them!

① Use File – Save As File...

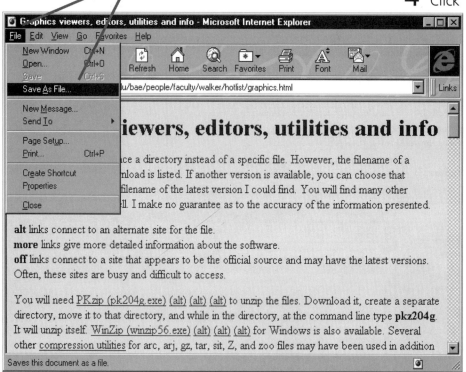

Graphics viewers, editors, utilities and info - Microsoft Internet Explorer

File Edit View Go Favorites Help

New Window Ctrl+N
Open... Ctrl+O
Save Ctrl+S
Save As File...

New Message...
Send To

Page Setup...
Print... Ctrl+P

Create Shortcut
Properties

Close

...u/bae/people/faculty/walker/hotlist/graphics.html

...iewers, editors, utilities and info

...ce a directory instead of a specific file. However, the filename of a ...nload is listed. If another version is available, you can choose that ...filename of the latest version I could find. You will find many other ...ll. I make no guarantee as to the accuracy of the information presented.

alt links connect to an alternate site for the file.
more links give more detailed information about the software.
off links connect to a site that appears to be the official source and may have the latest versions. Often, these sites are busy and difficult to access.

You will need PKzip (pk204g.exe) (alt) (alt) (alt) to unzip the files. Download it, create a separate directory, move it to that directory, and while in the directory, at the command line type **pkz204g**. It will unzip itself. WinZip (winzip56.exe) (alt) (alt) (alt) for Windows is also available. Several other compression utilities for arc, arj, gz, tar, sit, Z, and zoo files may have been used in addition

Saves this document as a file.

Tip

The History Folder tends to get rather full. If you find a page that you want to read off-line, it may be simpler to save it as a named file than to hunt for it in the History Folder.

□ **Opening filed pages**

5 Open the **File** menu and select **Open**

6 Click **Browse**.

7 Go to the right folder.

8 Select the file.

9 Click **Open**, then back at the Open panel, click **OK**.

③ Select the folder

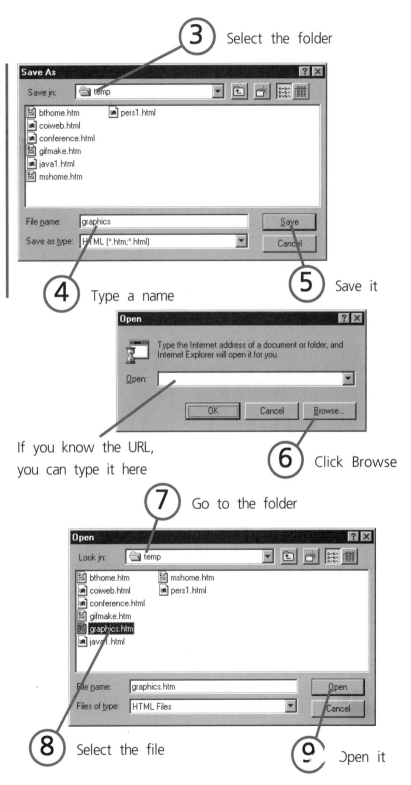

Save As

Save in: temp

- bthome.htm
- coiweb.html
- conference.html
- gifmake.htm
- java1.html
- mshome.htm
- pers1.html

File name: graphics

Save as type: HTML (*.htm;*.html)

Save

Cancel

④ Type a name

⑤ Save it

Open

Type the Internet address of a document or folder, and Internet Explorer will open it for you.

Open:

OK   Cancel   Browse...

If you know the URL, you can type it here

⑥ Click Browse

⑦ Go to the folder

Open

Look in: temp

- bthome.htm
- coiweb.html
- conference.html
- gifmake.htm
- graphics.htm
- java1.html
- mshome.htm
- pers1.html

File name: graphics.htm

Files of type: HTML Files

Open

Cancel

⑧ Select the file

⑨ Open it

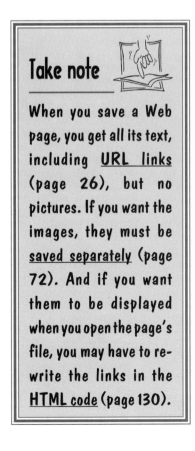

Take note

When you save a Web page, you get all its text, including **URL links** (page 26), but no pictures. If you want the images, they must be **saved separately** (page 72). And if you want them to be displayed when you open the page's file, you may have to re-write the links in the **HTML code** (page 130).

Summary

- There's a lot of **jargon** around on the Net. Some of it is essential, some of it is fun, and some is designed to confuse newcomers!

- Every page on the World WIde Web, and every file on the Internet has a **Uniform Resource Locator** (URL) that tells you how and where it can be found.

- **Hypertext** creates the links between pages on the World Wide Web.

- For faster surfing, you can opt not to **load in images**. Sometimes you need to see the images, either for their own interest or for the links that they carry.

- **Image maps** are pictures containing a number of embedded links. They are more attractive, but far slower alternatives to simple contents lists.

- If you know the URL of a Web page, you can go direct to it using the **Open Location** command.

- The **History Folder** keeps a record of where you have been, providing a simple means of returning to a site.

- Web pages can be **saved as file**s and read off-line. Only the text of pages is saved by this. If the images are wanted, they must be saved separately.

3 Starting to explore

Microsoft Home

The Links buttons and the Microsoft on the Web menu link to you seven places on the Microsoft site, from which to start your browsing.

● Microsoft's pages are highly graphic and slow to download on the first visit. However, if you revisit while the images are still in your Temporary Files store, downloading will be much quicker.

The **Help Topics** are on your machine
The **Web Tutorial** is on-line at Microsft

③ Select Help – Microsoft on the Web – Home Page

1 If you are not on-line, connect now.

2 If **Show pictures** is off, use **View – Options** and turn them on.

3 Open the **Help** menu, point to **Microsoft on the Web** and select **Microsoft Home Page**.

or

4 Click the Microsoft Link button.

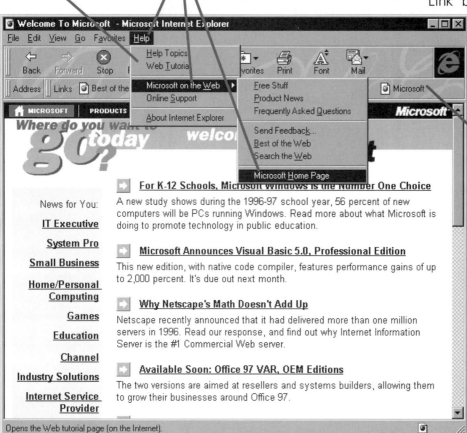

④ Click the link

Exploring at Microsoft

Tip

Explorer's Search button takes you directly to the main Microsoft Search facility (page 45).

There are hundreds of links in Microsoft's pages. You will find them embedded in the text, arranged in menus, listed down the side of pages and set in buttons at the top of the page. These button links connect to key places.

From **Exploring** you can head off in either of two directions:

- **Find It Fast** is a simple but comprehensive search system. Use it to find software (page 40), people (page 42) and to track down ideas and information.

- **The Best of the Web** is a catalogue of selected links, grouped under topic headings.

Read today's hot topic

Select a heading to start a search – see next page for more

Click here to find people (page 42)

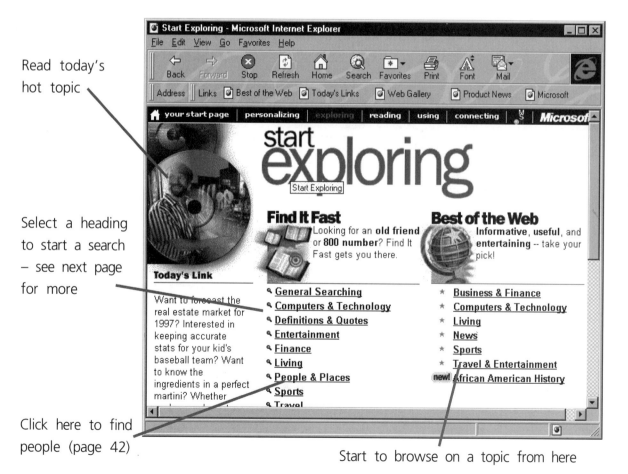

Start to browse on a topic from here

Find It Fast

Though there is cut-throat competition between suppliers of services and solutions, there is also a lot of co-operation. You can see this in *Find It Fast*. In each category you can search some of the best specialist sites on the Web, as well as relevant parts of the Microsoft site. In Computers & Technology, for instance, you can search the three top shareware sites (page 76).

Basic steps

1 At the **Exploring** page, select a Find It Fast category.

2 Click on a name to go to a search panel.

3 Enter the word(s) to search for.

4 Click **Search**.

(1) Select a catgeory

(2) Choose where to search

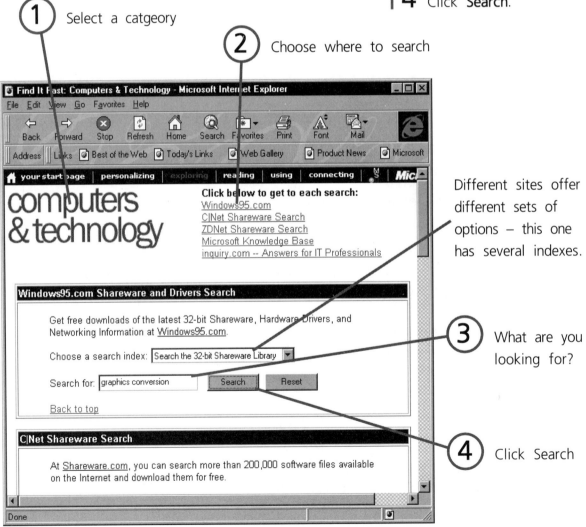

Different sites offer different sets of options – this one has several indexes.

(3) What are you looking for?

(4) Click Search

5 At the results page, click to follow up any promising link.

or

6 Start a new search.

Even if the search does not find exactly what you want, it may well take you to a page that has relevant links or a site with other interesting areas to explore.

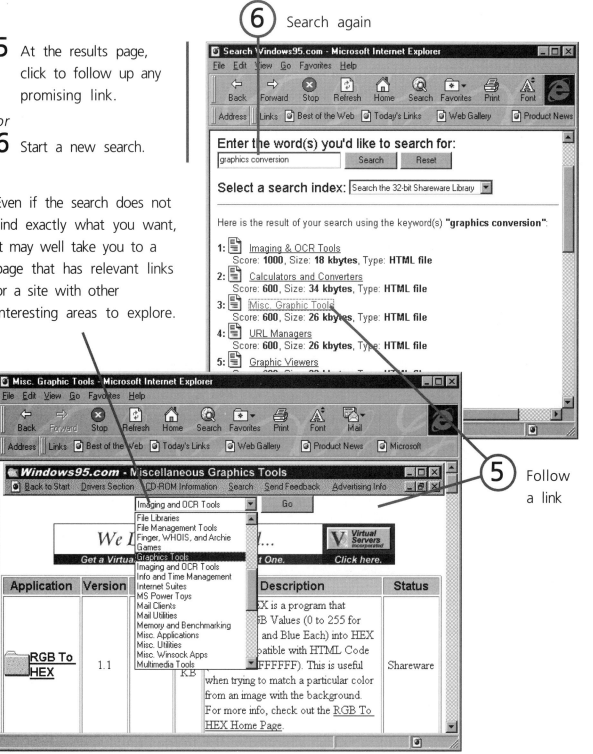

⑥ Search again

⑤ Follow a link

People

Finding people on the Internet can be very difficult. Users get on-line through hundreds of access providers or thousands of businesses – and there is no one controlling organisation. However, there are sites that are compiling directories of e-mail addresses, and one of the best of these can be reached from the Exploring page.

● Don't expect too much from this. You are more likely to succeed if the person is in the States or uses one of the major access providers.

● There's more about e-mail addresses on page 92.

There's more about e-mail addresses on page 92.

Basic steps

❏ **Finding people**

1 At the **Exploring** page, click on **People and Places** in Find It Fast.

2 Click E-Mail Addresses.

3 Enter the **name**.

4 Enter the **domain** (the firm's or provider's name), if known.

5 Click **Search**.

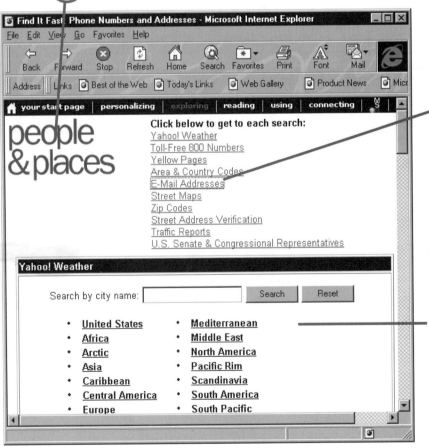

① Go to People & Places

② Click E-Mail Addresses

You can get other information here, including Weather reports, and US Zip codes and phone numbers.

6 If you get too few – or too many – results, go to **WhoWhere** to run an advanced search.

7 **Search by Location** to find a known person; or search by School, Affiliation or Interests to find new pen-pals.

③ Who?

④ Where?

⑤ Click Search

⑥ Try at WhoWhere

⑦ Enter known details

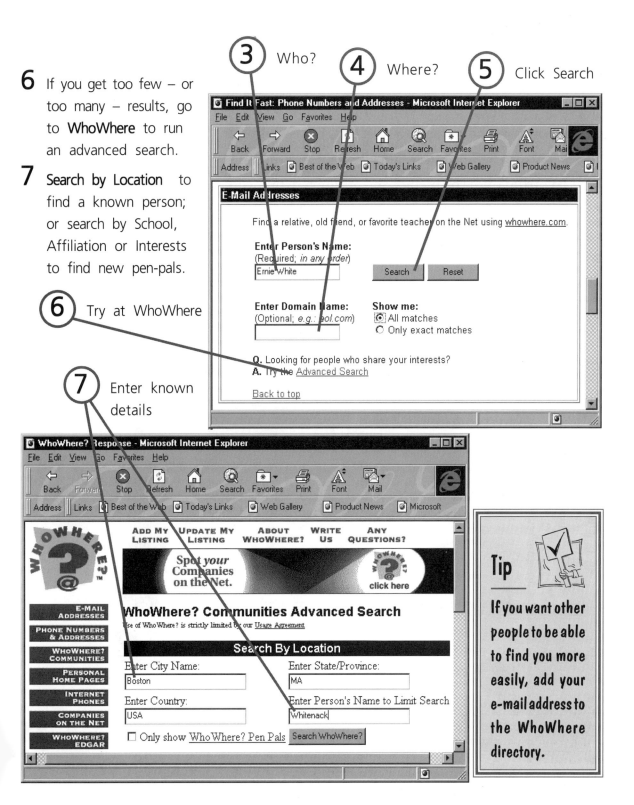

Find It Fast: Phone Numbers and Addresses - Microsoft Internet Explorer

File Edit View Go Favorites Help

Back Forward Stop Refresh Home Search Favorites Print Font Mail

Address Links Best of the Web Today's Links Web Gallery Product News

E-Mail Addresses

Find a relative, old friend, or favorite teacher on the Net using whowhere.com.

Enter Person's Name:
(Required; *in any order*)
Ernie White

Search   Reset

Enter Domain Name:
(Optional; *e.g.: aol.com*)

Show me:
○ All matches
○ Only exact matches

Q. Looking for people who share your interests?
A. Try the Advanced Search

Back to top

WhoWhere? Response - Microsoft Internet Explorer

File Edit View Go Favorites Help

Back Forward Stop Refresh Home Search Favorites Print Font Mail

Address Links Best of the Web Today's Links Web Gallery Product News Microsoft

WHOWHERE?@™

ADD MY LISTING   UPDATE MY LISTING   ABOUT WHOWHERE?   WRITE US   ANY QUESTIONS?

Spot *your* Companies on the Net.

WHOWHERE?@ click here

E-MAIL ADDRESSES
PHONE NUMBERS & ADDRESSES
WHOWHERE? COMMUNITIES
PERSONAL HOME PAGES
INTERNET PHONES
COMPANIES ON THE NET
WHOWHERE? EDGAR

WhoWhere? Communities Advanced Search

Use of WhoWhere? is strictly limited by our Usage Agreement

Search By Location

Enter City Name:
Boston

Enter State/Province:
MA

Enter Country:
USA

Enter Person's Name to Limit Search
Whitenack

☐ Only show WhoWhere? Pen Pals   Search WhoWhere?

Tip

If you want other people to be able to find you more easily, add your e-mail address to the WhoWhere directory.

43

The Web Gallery

Basic steps

1 Click **Web Gallery** in Explorer's Links.

2 Click an icon or a text link to get your stuff.

The Web Gallery is a great source of material for any Web builder – experienced or novice.

- If you don't have a clue about how to lay out your pages, try some of the style sheets.

- If you have got the basic page organised, but want to give it some zing, add some ready made sounds, images, ActiveX controls or Java applets.

- And for the DIY Web author, there are the tools to help you create your own pages and the zingy things to put on them.

Tip

There's a lot more about creating Web pages in Chapter 9.

① Click Web Gallery

② Click the icons or links

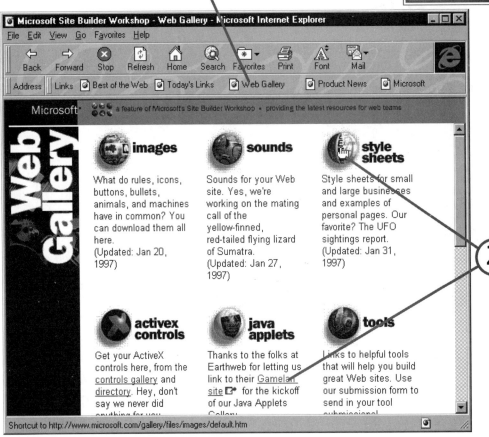

Basic steps

1 Click the **Search** in Explorer's toolbar.

2 Enter a word or phrase.

3 Select a **search engine**.

4 Click **Search**.

❑ You should get a list of pages containing the search item.

5 If you decide that you prefer one engine, click **Set Default** so it is selected for next time.

Search

If you are looking for something specific, try a Search. Some of the best search engines (systems that index and search the Internet) can be reached from here.

You may be lucky, but don't expect too much from this. A simple search does not always work that well and different engines produce different results. To search efficiently, you need to go to the search sites (chapter 4).

③ Select an engine

① Click Search

④ Click Search

② Enter search word(s)

⑤ Set Default?

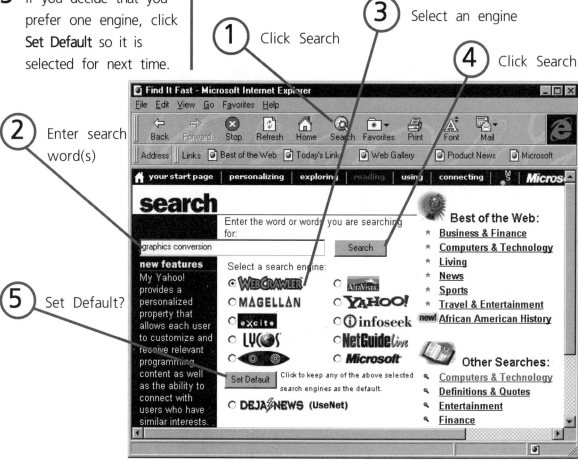

45

Your start page

Unless you have changed the Navigation options (page 13) you will have gone to this page at the start of every session. The page has a unique feature. Although it is at Microsoft, you can decide (much of) its content using the Personalizing routines. You can include the latest news, views and links from many sources, and have your favourite search engines to hand.

I have left the Start page until the end of this section because it is best tackled after you have a reasonable grasp of what's available, and have tried out the various search engines.

Basic steps

1 Click the **Personalizing** button.

2 Select a topic from the **Step 1** list and wait until a set of options have downloaded into the **Step 2** area.

3 Select the provider, search engine or other option under **Step 2**.

4 Click **Next**.

① Click Personalizing

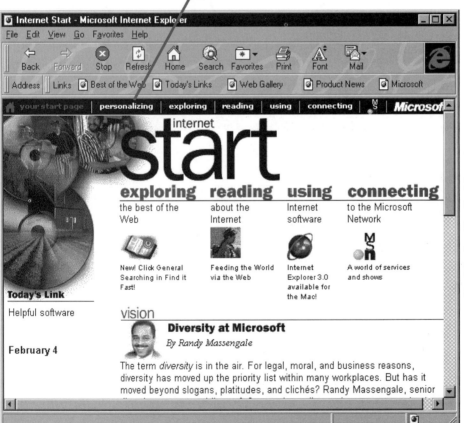

The top part of your start page carries a standard set of useful links and articles – the personal touches are added below.

5 Repeat Basic steps 2 to 4 for those topics that you want to include.

6 Click **Finish** and wait.

7 You will be sent the file **setiereg.reg** – save it to disk.

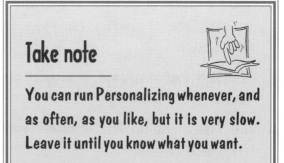

Take note

You can run Personalizing whenever, and as often, as you like, but it is very slow. Leave it until you know what you want.

② Pick a topic   ③ Set the option   ④ Click Next

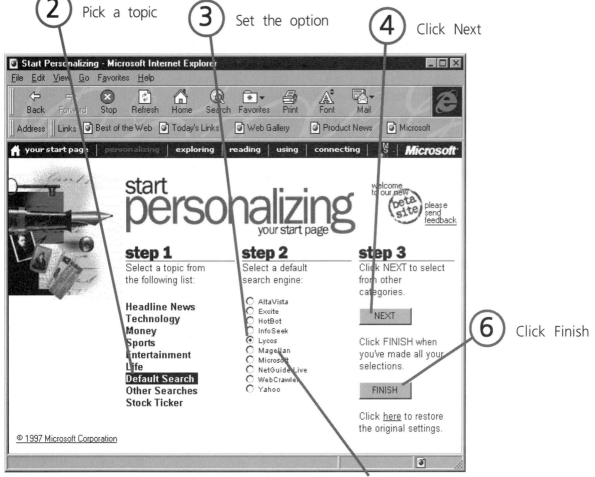

⑥ Click Finish

We'll look at some of these search engines more closely in chapter 4.

Summary

- There is loads of material at **Microsoft**'s site – though its heavy use of graphics can make browsing there very slow!

- The **Start Exploring** page is a good place from which to start your browsing.

- Use **Find It Fast** to find software, information and much else besides.

- You can track down long-lost friends and relatives (if they are on the Net) through the **People** page.

- The **Web Gallery** has a large collection of images, applets and ideas for you to use on your Web pages.

- If you are looking for specific information, you can find it faster by a **Search**, rather than browsing.

- You can link to the leading **search engines** from Microsoft's Search page.

- You can **personalise the Start page** at Microsoft.

4 Search engines

Alta Vista

Search enthusiasts generally rate Alta Vista as the best search engine around today. It is certainly extremely comprehensive and covers a huge proportion of the Internet's resources, yet is very easy to use.

A simple Alta Vista search, run from the Microsoft Search page, will tend to throw up thousands of 'hits' (matching pages). To filter these down to a manageable number, you must do an Advanced search.

Here, as at many search sites, you can use the operators:

AND   every word must match to produce a hit

OR   any matching word will produce a hit

Alta Vista also has its own special NOT NEAR operator.

You can also set a Ranking Criteria – insisting that a certain word must be included. This works like an AND operator, and is very effective in filtering the hits.

1 Start from Microsoft's search page.

2 Check the number of hits, and if there are only a few dozen, see what you have got.

3 Click **Advanced Search**.

4 Enter the words, using **AND** and **OR** as appropriate.

5 Enter a **Ranking Criteria**, if wanted.

6 If you want material from a certain time, set the **date limits**.

7 Click **Submit Advanced Query**.

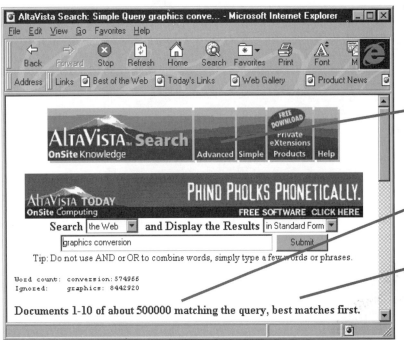

③ Click Advanced Search

② Too many hits?

As you get the best matches first, you might just find what you want in the top 10 hits.

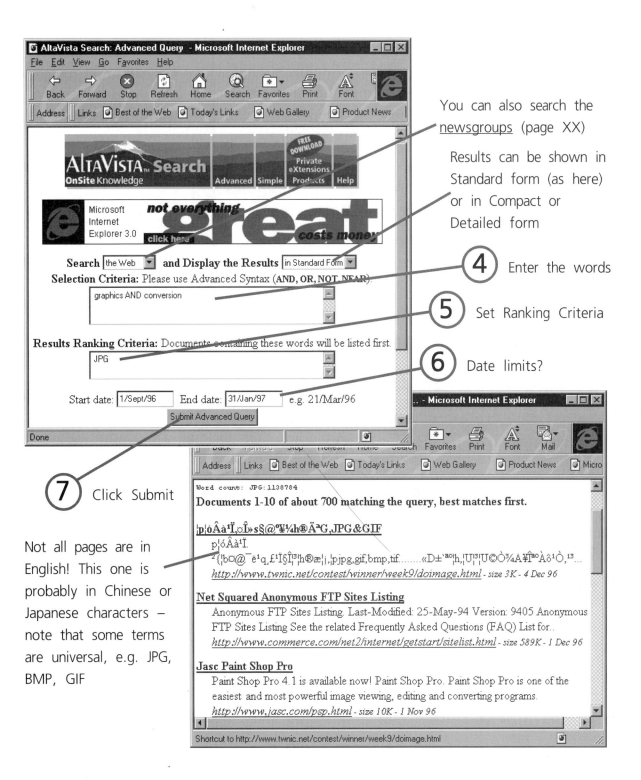

You can also search the <u>newsgroups</u> (page XX)

Results can be shown in Standard form (as here) or in Compact or Detailed form

④ Enter the words

⑤ Set Ranking Criteria

⑥ Date limits?

⑦ Click Submit

Not all pages are in English! This one is probably in Chinese or Japanese characters – note that some terms are universal, e.g. JPG, BMP, GIF

Excite

Excite's search facility is only one of the services that it provides to the Internet. There is also a catalogue, which contains probably the most comprehensive set of *reviewed* sites on the Web. These brief, but thoughtful, reviews make this one of the best places to start browsing.

When entering your search words, if you type '+' at the start, the word *must* be matched. e.g. '*+graphics +conversion*' is the same as '*graphics AND conversion*'

At Excite you can search through their reviews and newsgroup (page 106) articles, as well as the Web.

Basic steps

1 Run an **Excite Search** from **Microsoft**, or go directly to:
www.excite.com

2 Select where to search.

3 Type the search words using '+' if the word must be matched.

4 Click **Search**.

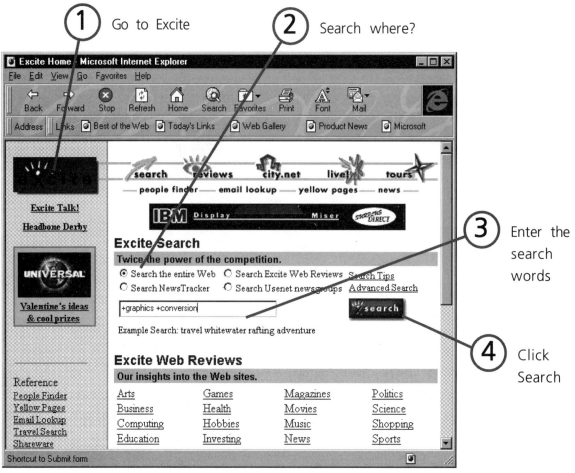

① Go to Excite

② Search where?

③ Enter the search words

④ Click Search

Excite has excellent reference facilities

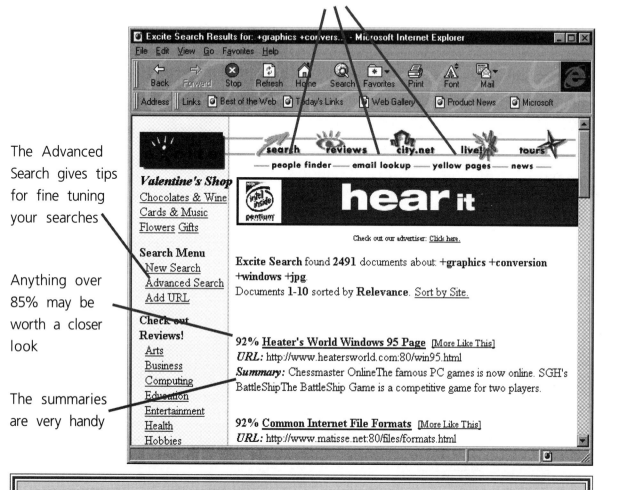

The Advanced Search gives tips for fine tuning your searches

Anything over 85% may be worth a closer look

The summaries are very handy

Take note

A search for 'graphics conversion' produced 1.5 million hits at Excite! Even tightly specified searches tend to produce lots. Fortunately, they are listed in order of relevance. A search for '+graphics +conversion +windows +jpg' produced 2,500 hits, but there were many useful sites in the first ten. Though Heater's World Windows (games) page came top, Paint Shop Pro — the great graphics conversion shareware program — was number five in this case.

Infoseek

The best way to find anything at Infoseek is to run a series of searches, each based on the results of the last, focusing steadily in on the material that you want. If you are looking, say, for 'graphics conversion shareware', don't start by entering all three words – it will simply find pages that contain any one of the three. Start with a single word, and narrow the search one word at a time.

When tested, 'graphics' produced over 700,000 hits! Filtered first with 'conversion' then 'windows' reduced these to 790. Further filtering with 'jpg' brought this down to 34 – and the first hit was Paint Shop Pro!

1 Start Searching from **Microsoft**, or go to: **www.infoseek.com**

2 Run a simple search.

3 Go to the bottom of the page and enter a focusing word.

4 Select **Search only these results**.

5 Click **Seek**.

6 Repeat 3 to 5 to get a reasonably-sized set.

① Go to Infoseek

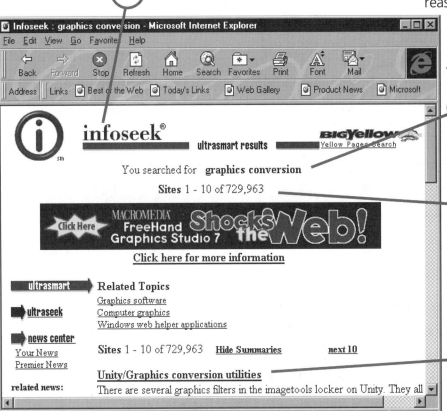

② Run a simple search

A search for 'graphics conversion', finds 730,000 pages with either 'graphics' or 'conversion'.

Those at the top of the list have both.

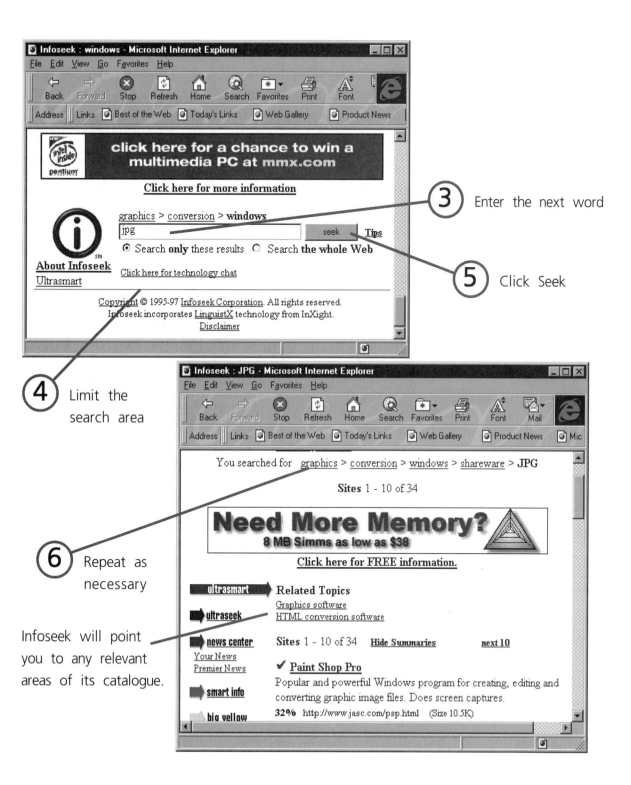

③ Enter the next word

⑤ Click Seek

④ Limit the search area

⑥ Repeat as necessary

Infoseek will point you to any relevant areas of its catalogue.

55

Lycos

If you can't find it through Lycos, it probably doesn't exist. At the time of testing, Lycos had indexed over 66 million Web pages! Despite this size, results are returned in a few seconds, and if you define your search properly, you won't get swamped by hundreds of references.

Lycos has an unusual set of search options. You can set it to *match 2 terms* (or 3, 4, 5, 6 or 7), as well as the more normal *match all* (AND) or *match any* (OR). You can also set the closeness of match – from *loose* to *strong*. Strong matching will filter out irrelevant sites, though if you are looking for something esoteric, a loose match will help to pick up any passing references.

1 Go to **Lycos** from **Search**, or directly at: www.lycos.com

2 Click **New Search**.

3 Click **Custom Search**.

4 Select the search area.

5 Enter the term(s) to search **for**.

6 Set the **Search Options**.

7 Set the **Display Options** if required.

8 Click **Go Get It!**

 Click New Search

 Go to Lycos

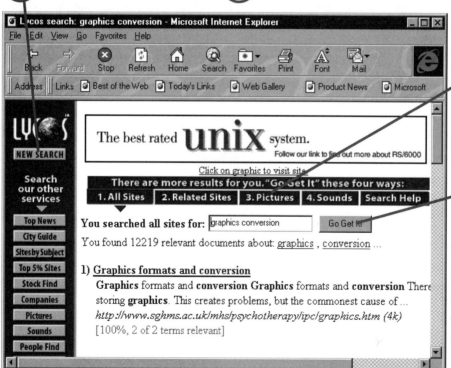

Use Related Sites, Pictures or Sounds for a more focused search.

You can do a simple search from this page

The People Finder is excellent – in fact, most of Lycos' other services are worth exploring.

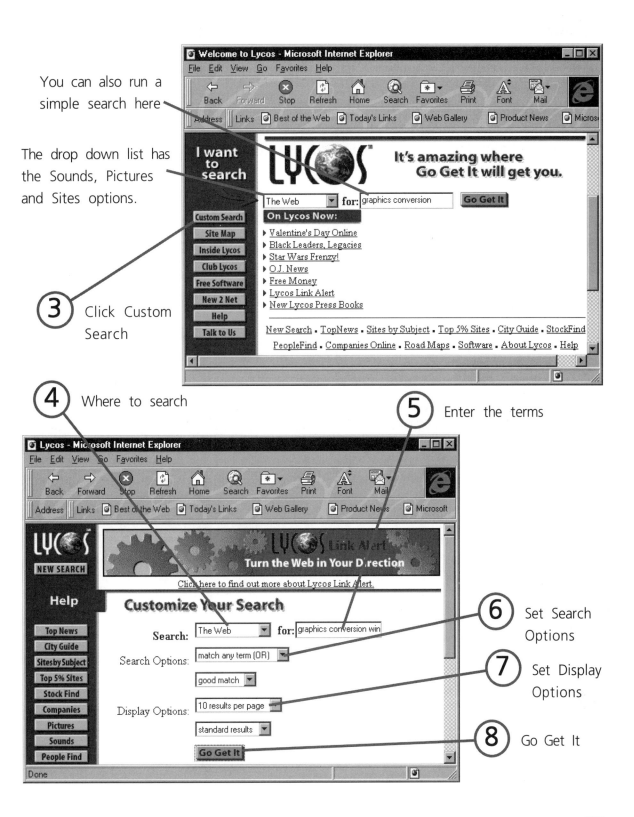

You can also run a simple search here

The drop down list has the Sounds, Pictures and Sites options.

③ Click Custom Search

④ Where to search

⑤ Enter the terms

⑥ Set Search Options

⑦ Set Display Options

⑧ Go Get It

Magellan

Magellan is notable for its *Green Light* sites – ones that have been certified as suitable for 'family viewing'. Sites are also reviewed and rated for the quality of their content. Not all sites have been reviewed – the sheer size and explosive growth of the Internet make this impossible – but Magellan do seem to cover the more significant ones.

When searching here, you can restrict your search to reviewed sites, and then to the more highly rated. You can also use the logical operators AND (every word must match) and OR (any matching word).

Basic steps

1 Go to **Magellan** from **Search**, or directly to: www.mckinley.com

2 Enter the word(s) to search for.

3 Click **Options**.

4 Restrict the **sites** to be searched, if desired.

1 Go to Magellan

2 Enter the word(s)

3 Click Options

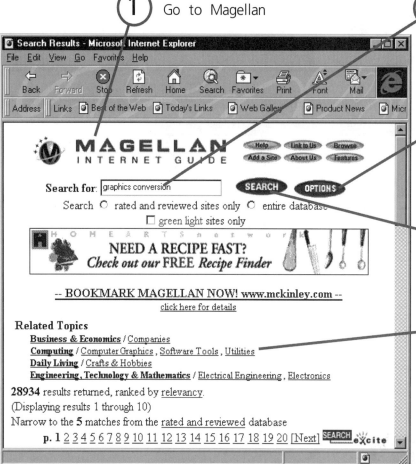

You can run a simple search directly from here

These lead to sections in the Magellan directory

5 Set the **Rating** – *four stars only* searches a small set of good sites.

6 Select **AND** or **OR** between the words.

7 Click **Submit choices**.

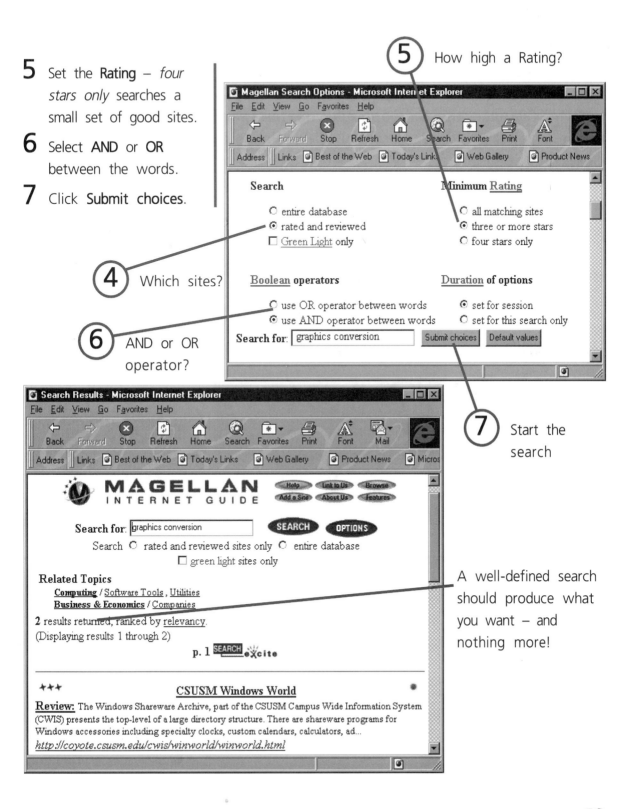

⑤ How high a Rating?

Magellan Search Options - Microsoft Internet Explorer

File Edit View Go Favorites Help

Back Forward Stop Refresh Home Search Favorites Print Font

Address   Links 🔘 Best of the Web 🔘 Today's Links 🔘 Web Gallery 🔘 Product News

Search

○ entire database
◉ rated and reviewed
□ Green Light only

Minimum Rating

○ all matching sites
◉ three or more stars
○ four stars only

Boolean operators

○ use OR operator between words
◉ use AND operator between words

Duration of options

◉ set for session
○ set for this search only

Search for: graphics conversion   [Submit choices] [Default values]

④ Which sites?

⑥ AND or OR operator?

⑦ Start the search

Search Results - Microsoft Internet Explorer

File Edit View Go Favorites Help

Back Forward Stop Refresh Home Search Favorites Print Font Mail

Address   Links 🔘 Best of the Web 🔘 Today's Links 🔘 Web Gallery 🔘 Product News 🔘 Micros

MAGELLAN INTERNET GUIDE

Help Link to Us Browse
Add a Site About Us Features

Search for: graphics conversion   **SEARCH** **OPTIONS**

Search ○ rated and reviewed sites only ○ entire database
□ green light sites only

Related Topics
Computing / Software Tools , Utilities
Business & Economics / Companies

2 results returned, ranked by relevancy.
(Displaying results 1 through 2)
p. 1 [SEARCH] eXcite

★★★   **CSUSM Windows World**   ●

Review: The Windows Shareware Archive, part of the CSUSM Campus Wide Information System (CWIS) presents the top-level of a large directory structure. There are shareware programs for Windows accessories including specialty clocks, custom calendars, calculators, ad...
http://coyote.csusm.edu/cwis/winworld/winworld.html

A well-defined search should produce what you want – and nothing more!

Yahoo

Yahoo was one of the first, and is still one of the best Internet directories. It is a great place to start browsing – but whereabouts within Yahoo should you start? For most topics, it is fairly clear where they will fit in Yahoo's categories. Sometimes it is not so obvious, and that is where the search facility comes in handy. Its main value is in locating links within Yahoo.

(1) Run a Yahoo Search

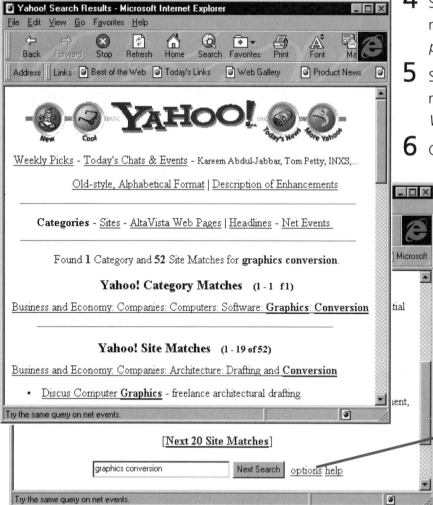

Click options (2)

Basic steps

1 Run a **Yahoo Search** from Microsoft.

2 If you don't find what you want, go to the bottom of the page and click **options**.

3 Enter the word(s) to search for.

4 Select the method – note the useful *exact phrase match*.

5 Select the search area – normally *Categories* or *Web Sites*.

6 Click **Search**.

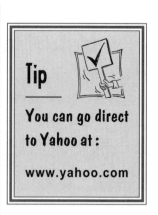

Tip

You can go direct to Yahoo at :

www.yahoo.com

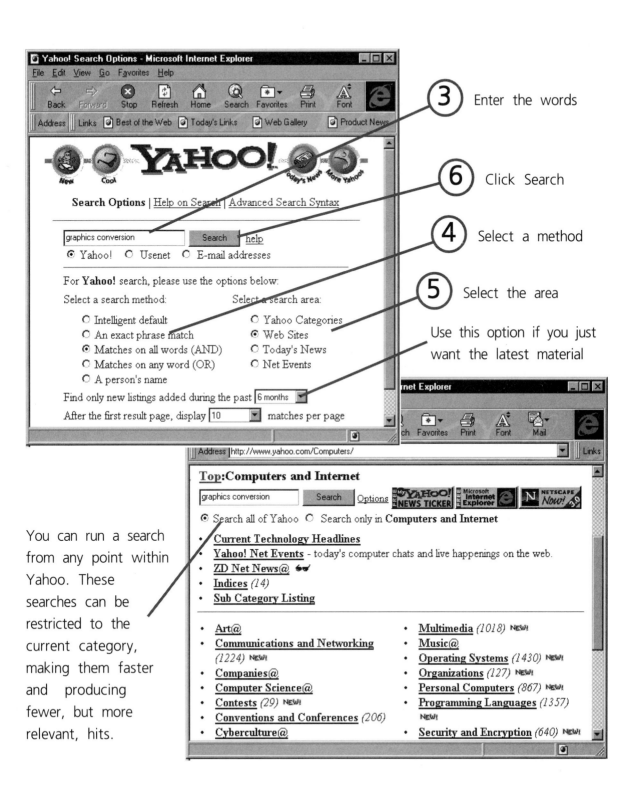

③ Enter the words

⑥ Click Search

④ Select a method

⑤ Select the area

Use this option if you just want the latest material

You can run a search from any point within Yahoo. These searches can be restricted to the current category, making them faster and producing fewer, but more relevant, hits.

Summary

- ❏ **Alta Vista** offers extremely comprehensive coverage of the Net and simple, but powerful search facilities.

- ❏ **Excite** reviews more sites than any other service.

- ❏ The **Infoseek** search engine lets you focus in on pages through a series of filters.

- ❏ **Lycos** offers a range of excellent facilities, alongside its search engine.

- ❏ **Magellan** gives sites star ratings and **Green Lights** to those suitable for family viewing.

- ❏ **Yahoo** is probably the Web's biggest and best directory.

5 Favorites

Favorite places

Some good places are easy to find; others you discover over a long and painful search or by sheer chance. If you want to return to these pages in future, the simple solution is to add them to your Favorites. This stores the title and URL of the page as an *Internet Shortcut*, and puts the title onto the Favorites menu.

- When you want to go back to a page in a later session, you can simply pick it from the Favorites menu.

- You must have the page open to be able to add it to the Favorites – but you can do this off-line by opening the page from the History Folder (page 32).

- The Favorites are stored in a folder (in \Windows). If you have a lot of entries, you can organise them (page 66) into new folders within this, creating sub-menus of Favorites.

The toolbar button and menu item do exactly the same job.

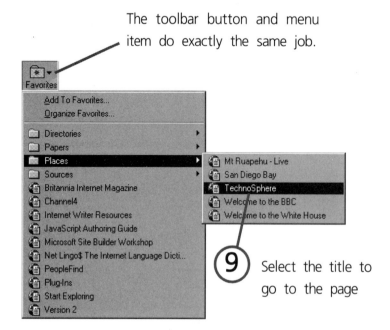

9 Select the title to go to the page

Basic steps

❑ Adding Favorites

1 Find a good page!

2 Open **Favorites**.

3 Select **Add to Favorites**.

4 Edit the name if necessary.

5 To add it to the main menu, click **OK**.

or

6 To store it in a folder, click **Create in>>**.

7 Select the folder.

8 Click **OK**.

❑ Using Favorites

9 Open **Favorites** and select the page title.

Take note

Links in the History Folder eventually disappear as old ones are removed to make way for new ones. Links stored as Favorites remain there, unless you decide to remove them.

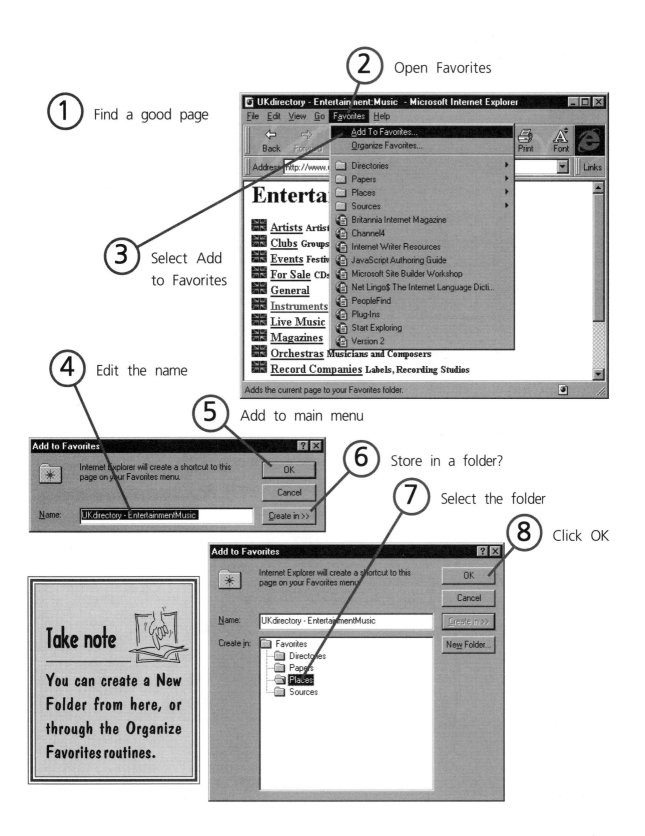

① Find a good page

② Open Favorites

③ Select Add to Favorites

④ Edit the name

⑤ Add to main menu

⑥ Store in a folder?

⑦ Select the folder

⑧ Click OK

Take note

You can create a New Folder from here, or through the Organize Favorites routines.

65

Organising Favorites

The more titles you have on the menu, the harder it is to spot one. Once you have more than a dozen or so, they need organising. If you **Organize Favorites**, you can group them into folders, which then appear as items on the Favorites menu and lead to submenus.

Before you do this, work out which ones have something in common, and what you would call their folders. Odds and ends can be left on the main menu and grouped later.

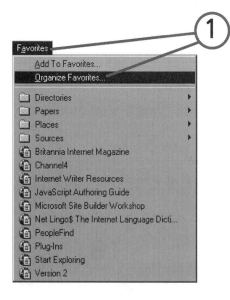

① Use Favorites — Organize Favorites

Basic steps

1 Open the **Favorites** menu and select **Organize Favorites**.

2 Click [icon] to create a new folder in the current one.

3 Change the name from *New Folder* to a more meaningful one – this goes on the Favorites menu.

② Click the New Folder button

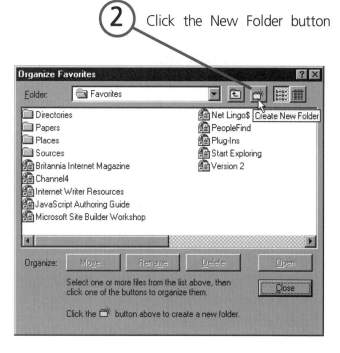

Tip

If you want to create a multi-level menu, double-click on the first level folder to open it and create the new folder in there.

③ Give it a meaningful name

Simple list

Detailed list

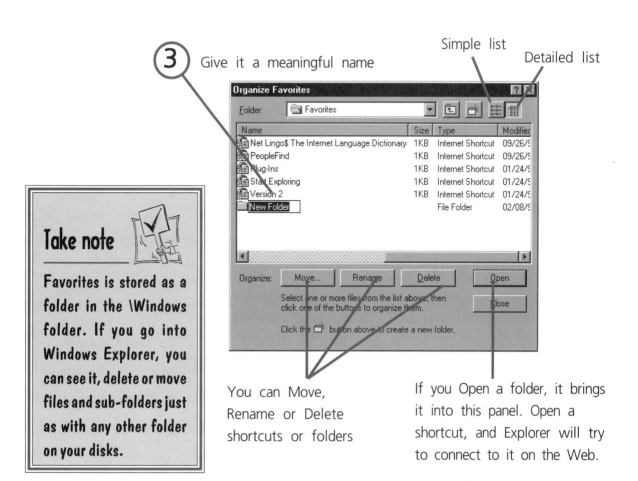

You can Move, Rename or Delete shortcuts or folders

If you Open a folder, it brings it into this panel. Open a shortcut, and Explorer will try to connect to it on the Web.

Favorites is just another folder to Windows Explorer

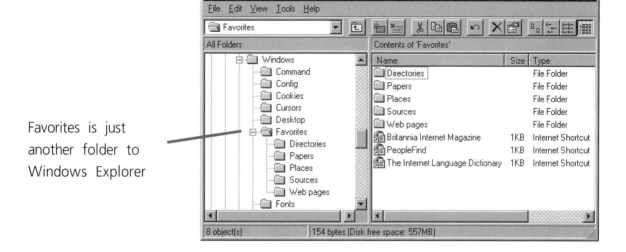

Moving shortcuts

Once you have created your new folders, you can move shortcuts out of the main Favorites folder and into the new ones – i.e. off the main menu and into submenus.

● If the shortcut and its target folder are both visible in the panel, you can move a shortcut by dragging it.

● If you are trying to move a shortcut from one folder into another, or to move a whole folder from within another one, then you must use the Move button.

● To move several shortcuts together, use the [Ctrl] or [Shift] keys, as in Windows Explorer:

❑ To select shortcuts scattered over the display, hold down [Ctrl] and click on those you want.

❑ To select a block of shortcuts, click on the topmost one, hold down [Shift] and click on the last one in the block.

❑ **Move by dragging**

1 Select the shortcut(s) using **[Ctrl]** or **[Shift]** as necessary.

2 Hold down the left mouse button and drag the shortcuts across the display until the target folder is highlighted.

3 Release the mouse button.

❑ **The Move button**

4 Select the shortcut(s).

5 Click **Move**.

6 Select the target folder.

7 Click **OK**.

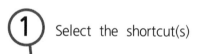

① Select the shortcut(s)

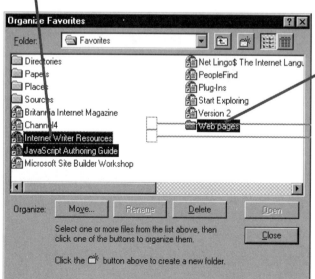

② Drag to the target

③ Release the mouse button

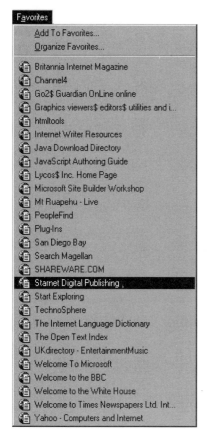

4 Select the shortcut(s)

6 Select the target

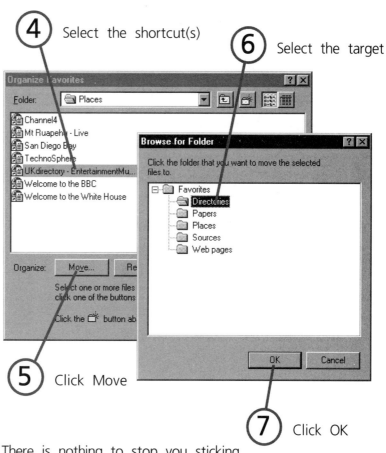

5 Click Move

7 Click OK

There is nothing to stop you sticking all your shortcuts on the main menu...

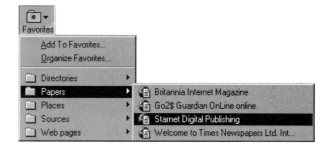

...but an organised set of folders makes it much easier to find things.

Summary

- ❑ If you add a site to your **Favorite places**, you will have an easy means to get back to it another day.

- ❑ Favorites can be **organised into folders**, so that they appear in submenus on the Favorite menu.

- ❑ Favorite take their names from the titles of pages. If these are not clear, you can **edit the name** as you add the page to your set.

- ❑ **New Favorites** can be added into a chosen folder.

- ❑ Favorites can be **moved** into different folders, just as files can be moved in Windows Explorer.

6 Files from the Web

Embedded images

There are four main ways in which you can get files through Explorer:

● Pictures and other files embedded in Web pages can be saved directly off the page.

● Pages may contain URL links to files. Software houses publish demos, beta-tests and shareware this way; specialist resource pages run by organisations and enthusiasts often have links to relevant files. These are easily <u>downloaded</u> (page 74).

● <u>FTP sites</u> (page 78) hold large stores of shareware and public domain files. Some of these sites are indexed and organised for easy access, with descriptions of the files; with others, you have to hunt through directories, with only the bare filenames to guide you.

● Files can also be sent to you via <u>e-mail</u> (page 98), by friends and colleagues around the world.

Picking files directly off the page is simplest, so that is where we will start.

Basic steps

1 Wait until the images are fully loaded.

2 Right click on the image to be saved.

3 Select **Save Picture As...** from the short menu.

4 Select a folder.

5 Change the filename if the orginal name does not identify the file clearly enough for you.

6 Click **Save**.

❑ Saving should be almost instantaneous as the data is already in your computer.

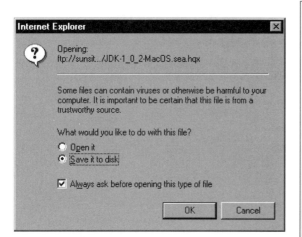

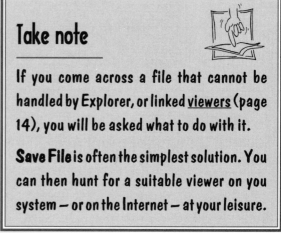

Take note

If you come across a file that cannot be handled by Explorer, or linked <u>viewers</u> (page 14), you will be asked what to do with it.

Save File is often the simplest solution. You can then hunt for a suitable viewer on you system – or on the Internet – at your leisure.

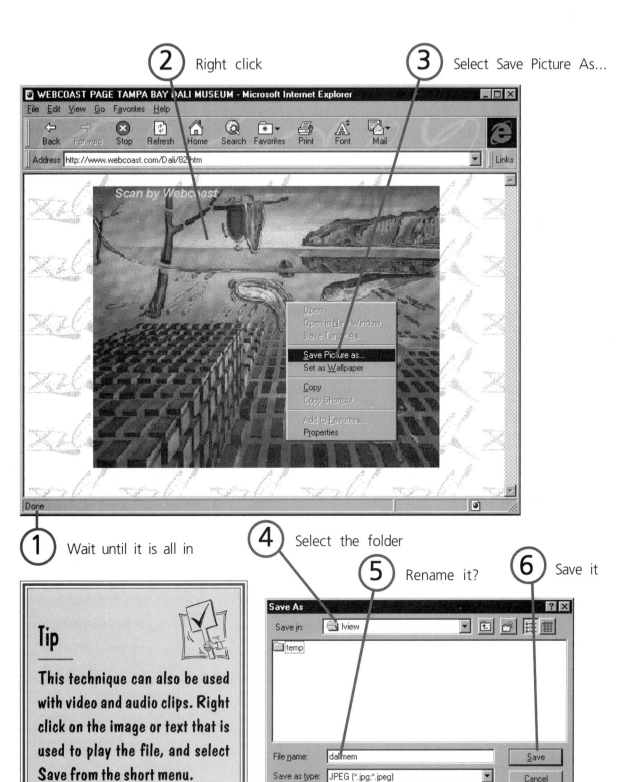

(2) Right click

(3) Select Save Picture As...

WEBCOAST PAGE TAMPA BAY DALI MUSEUM - Microsoft Internet Explorer

File Edit View Go Favorites Help

Back Forward Stop Refresh Home Search Favorites Print Font Mail

Address http://www.webcoast.com/Dali/82.htm

Scan by Webcoast

Open
Open in New Window
Save Target As...

Save Picture as...
Set as Wallpaper

Copy
Copy Shortcut

Add to Favorites...
Properties

Done

(1) Wait until it is all in

(4) Select the folder

(5) Rename it?

(6) Save it

Tip

This technique can also be used with video and audio clips. Right click on the image or text that is used to play the file, and select Save from the short menu.

Save As

Save in: lview

temp

File name: dalimem

Save as type: JPEG (*.jpg;*.jpeg)

Save

Cancel

Downloading linked files

Downloadable files are usually easy to identify. For a start – like all links – they will be underlined and in a different colour! The names may be shown in filename form, such as *bdk_beta.exe*, or as the program title, e.g. *Capture It!*

If you point to a filename, and look in the status line, you will see the URL. This will show you the nature of the link. This may be:

- directly to the *file*, shown by **ftp://** at the start and a filename at the end. e.g.

  ftp://mrcnext.cso.uiuc.edu/pub/win3/desktop/psp30.zip

  If the filename has the **.zip** extension, it is Zip-compressed, and will need WinZip to extract it. Those ending **.exe** are often also Zip-compressed, but are self-extracting.

- to an *FTP site*, shown by **ftp://** at the start and **/** at the end. e.g.

  ftp://gated.cornell.edu/pub/video/

  Before you follow this link, make a careful note of the filename as you will have to hunt for the file when you reach the FTP site.

- to a *page* which contains it, shown by **http://** at the start and **.html** or **.htm** at the end. e.g.

  http://pc.inrird.com/cgirend.html

  Once there, you should find download instructions.

Basic steps

1 Point to the link and read the URL in the status bar.

❑ **File URLs**

2 Click on the link.

3 When the Save dialog opens, select the folder as shown on page 73. Leave the original filename.

❑ **FTP site URLs**

4 Make a note of the filename.

5 Click on the link, then follow the steps for FTP sites on page 79.

Tip

If the lines to the site are busy, the download speed may be far too slow (under 1 Kb/sec). At times like this, it is often better to cancel the download, write down the URL, and try again later.

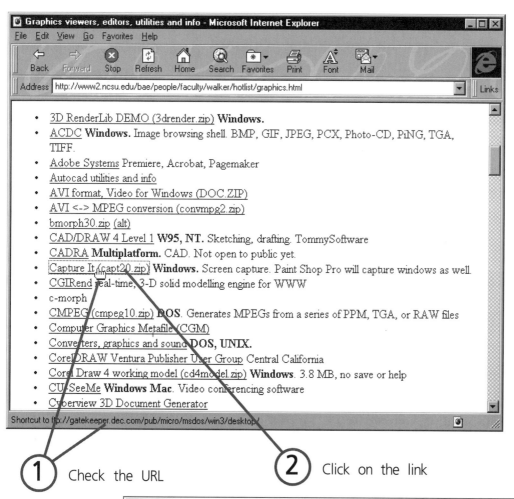

① Check the URL

② Click on the link

Tip

WinZip is the most widely used compression software for Windows and DOS files. You can get a copy from for the WinZip home page at:

http://www.winzip.com

For other compressed files you will need Stuffit Expander. Get a copy from:

http://www.aladdinsys.com

Shareware sites

There are literally megabytes of shareware (and freeware) programs available through the Web – and one of the best places is **shareware.com**. This is run by CNET which also provides a range of other services to Internet users.

● If you are looking for particular software – and know its name – use the Quick Search facility.

● If you are just starting to build your shareware collection, try the Most Popular selection.

1 Go to: **http:// www.shareware.com**

2 In the **Quick Search** slot type the (common) name of the program.

3 Select your operating system.

4 Click **Search** and wait.

5 Read the descriptions to find the right file.

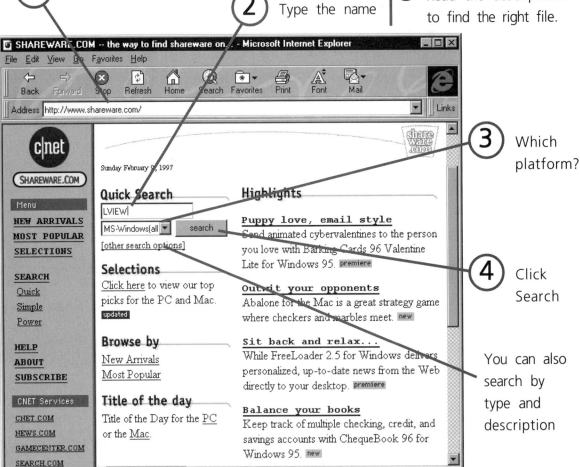

76

6 Click on the filename to start the download – saving the file as usual.

6 Click to download

5 Read about the files

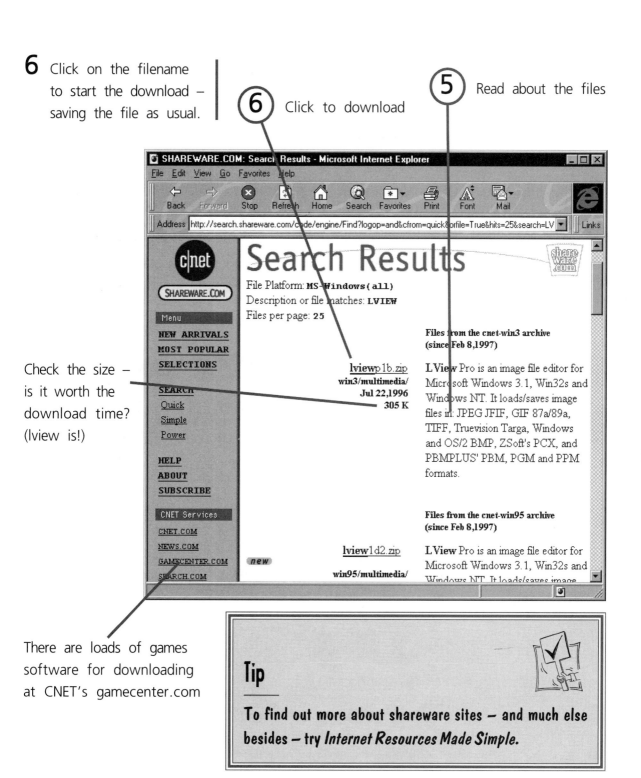

Check the size – is it worth the download time? (lview is!)

There are loads of games software for downloading at CNET's gamecenter.com

Tip

To find out more about shareware sites – and much else besides – try *Internet Resources Made Simple.*

FTP sites

There are thousands of FTP sites – stores of software, documents and other files that can be accessed using the File Transfer Protocol. Most universities, most Internet access and service providers, and many government and commercial organisations offer this facility.

At most sites, you get bare directory listings (see opposite). As these are plain text, you can browse through them quite quickly, but finding stuff can be difficult.

Some of the better sites, like Simtel.Net at Oakland University, have HTML front ends and well-indexed files. Heavy use of graphics can slow down your work here!

Tip

If you are looking for good software, try the Oak Software Repository at:

http://oak.oaklands.edu

This leads to the Virtual Software Library, Simtel and much more.

There is usually a README file – do read it!

Files – click
to download

Directory –
click to open

Filenames can also give a clue
to the type – notice the win32
and MacOS in these names

Take note

To find out where (almost) all the FTP sites are, go to:

http://hoohoo.ncsa.uiuc.edu/ftp

The Monster list has over 20 parts to it, and each part
is around 50Kb – that is over 1 Megabyte in total!

Searching with Archie

Before you can download a file, you have to know its name and where it is. This is when you need Archie.

Scattered over the Internet are a number of hosts that act as Archie servers. Each of these has a database of the directory listings of major FTP sites. An Archie server also has a program – called Archie – that can interrogate this database to locate files.

Search types

Archie can use one of four different matching methods as it searches its database.

Substring: Looks for the given string within the names of files and directories – and the more you can give, the better. For example, looking for a copy of Paint Shop Pro (the graphic conversion utility) with '**psp**' produces nearly 100 hits, including '**psp**lan.ps.Z', and 'crystalswa**psp**eedup.txt'. Trying with '**pspro**' gets around 20 hits, including 'XD**PSpro**to.h', 's**pspro**g.txt' and '**pspro**30.zip' – the one you want.

Substring (case sensitive): As substring, but matching lower/upper case characters exactly as given. '**pspro**' would not find 'XD**PSpro**to.h' (good), but equally, 'PSPRO' would find find '**pspro**30.zip' (bad).

Exact: Looks for an exact match (including case) for the given name. This is fast, but you must know exactly what you want. If you are looking for shareware or beta-test software, Exact may miss the latest version.

For example, the latest version of Explorer at the time of writing was '**msie30r.exe**', but searching for this now may give you an out of date copy. A substring search forf '**msie**' will be more productive.

Regex: Use *regular expressions* when matching. These are taken from the Unix utility *ed* (a text editor) and are similar to DOS wildcards. But not that similar – the differences are significant.

Regular expressions

The basic wildcard is '.' (dot), standing for any single character – the equivalent to '?' in MS-DOS. This was a rotten choice, as dot is an essential part of most filenames. If you want to use dot for its proper meaning – not as a wildcard – put a backslash in front of it, i.e. '\.'

'winzip\.exe' will find the file 'winzip.exe'

'winzip.exe' will look for 'winzipAexe', 'winzipBexe', etc. and probably find nothing!

'*' is a repeater, standing for any number of whatever character was written before it. 'A*' means any number of A's. Use '.*' to stand for any set of any characters – the equivalent of the simpler '*' in MS-DOS.

'babel.*txt' looks for files that start with 'babel', end with 'txt' and have something (or nothing) in between.

You can specify a set of alternative single characters by enclosing them in square brackets – '[...]'

'babel97[ab]\.txt' will find 'babel97a.txt' and 'babel97b.txt'

Ranges can be defined with '-', e.g. [A-F] is the same as [ABCDEF].

'^' at the start of a range means match characters that are *not* in the list, e.g. [^A-Z] means ignore all capitals.

Take note

Regular expressions are case-sensitive – capitals and lower case letters are treated as different characters. If in doubt about which to use for a search, try lower case first – filenames are generally written in lower case.

Archie Gateways

To run an Archie search from Explorer, go to Yahoo and select *Computers and Internet – Internet – Archie.* There you will find a number of links labelled *Archie Request Form* or *Archie Gateway.*

1 Go to an **Archie Gateway** or **Request Form.**

2 Enter your search string.

3 Select the **match type** – substring, regex or exact.

4 If the option is there, set the priority of the request – less urgent or 'nicer' requests let local users have first call on the server's activities.

5 Select your **server** – use the one closest to home if possible.

6 Restrict the **number of results** to 10 – 20.

7 **Submit** the search.

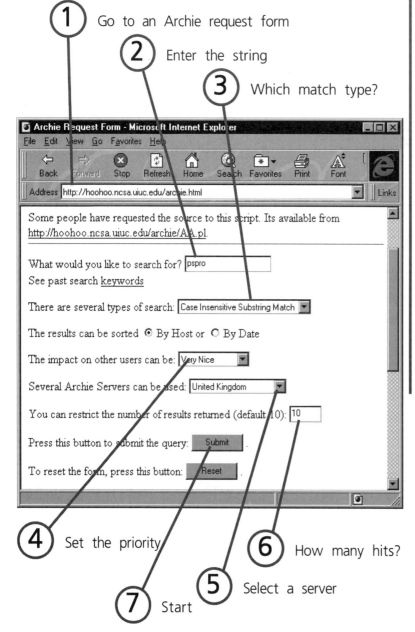

(1) Go to an Archie request form

(2) Enter the string

(3) Which match type?

Some people have requested the source to this script. Its available from http://hoohoo.ncsa.uiuc.edu/archie/AA.pl.

What would you like to search for? pspro
See past search keywords

There are several types of search: Case Insensitive Substring Match

The results can be sorted ⦿ By Host or ◯ By Date

The impact on other users can be: Very Nice

Several Archie Servers can be used: United Kingdom

You can restrict the number of results returned (default 10): 10

Press this button to submit the query: Submit

To reset the form, press this button: Reset

(4) Set the priority

(6) How many hits?

(5) Select a server

(7) Start

Take note

You will find variations in the appearance of Archie request forms, but they all work in the same way.

Files from an Archie Gateway

- ❏ Click on a filename to download the file.

- ❏ Click on a site or directory to jump there, so that you can browse for other files.

If your Archie search is productive, you will get a page or more listing the results. Here you will see the FTP sites, directories and name of the matching files. Normally all of these will be hyperlinked.

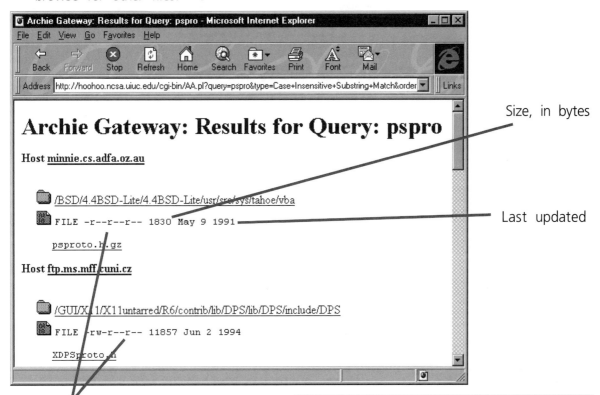

Size, in bytes

Last updated

Shows who can do what to the file. 'r' is permission to read (or download) the file; 'w' is for write (change or delete); 'x', if present, is execute permission. The first three letters are the owner's permissions; the next three those of the local group, the last three show what anyone can do. So, if it ends r-- you can download the file

Take note

There are Archie Request Forms at:

http://hoohoo.ncsa.uiuc.edu/archie.html

http://www.wg.omron.co.jp/AA-eng.html

http://www-ns.rutgers.edu/htbin/archie

Summary

- ❑ You can **save an image** – or other file – that is embedded in a page, by right-clicking on it and using the Save As option.

- ❑ If you want to **download a file** that is linked from a page, just click on the link.

- ❑ There are vast quantities of **shareware** available over the Internet. The best places to find it are at sites such as **shareware.com**.

- ❑ Many **FTP sites** are fairly hard to use as they are simply vast stores of files, with little or no guidance as to their nature. Fortunately, a growing number have added catalogues, with descriptions of the files, making the archives much more accessible.

- ❑ **Archie** is a combined program and database for finding files in FTP sites.

- ❑ You can reach Archie through **Gateways** on the Web.

7 Explorer Mail

The Mail Wizard

The first time that you try to use the Mail, a Wizard will run automatically. This will collect and install all the details that are needed to create the mail connection. You must have this information to hand:

● your e-mail account name – this should be the same as your user name, e.g. JoSmith

● your log-on password

● your e-mail name, e.g. JoSmith@mynet.co.uk

● the names of your service provider's Incoming and Outgoing Mail Servers – these may well be the same.

Basic steps

1 Open the **Go** menu, or click the **Mail** button, and select **Read Mail**.

2 Click **Next** to start the Wizard – and after each stage.

3 Enter your real name and e-mail address.

4 Enter the Mail Server names.

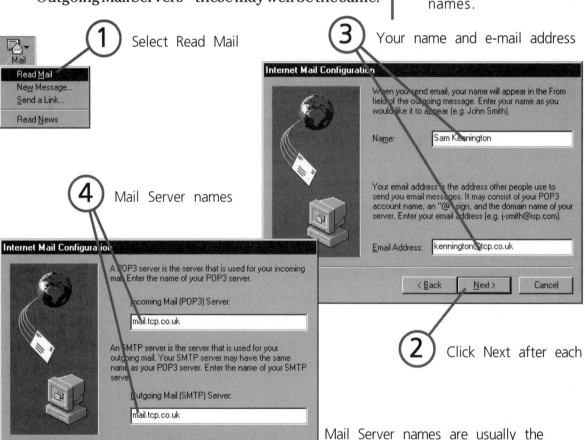

① Select Read Mail

③ Your name and e-mail address

④ Mail Server names

② Click Next after each

Mail Server names are usually the provider's name with mail at the start

5 Enter your e-mail account name and your password.

6 Select your connection method – for most people this will be *Use a modem.*

7 Click **Finish.**

8 Explorer will try to connect to your Mail Server. Enter your password again, and click **Save Password** – unless you want to enter it each time you log on for your mail.

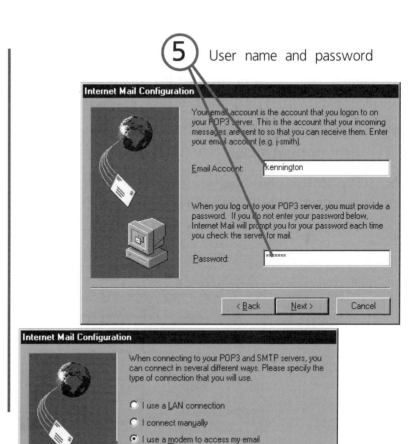

⑤ User name and password

⑥ How do you connect?

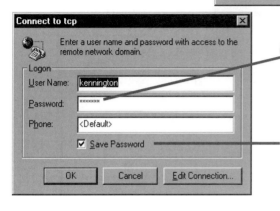

⑧ Enter the password again

If others use your computer – but not the Mail account – you may prefer not to save the password

The Mail window

This is where you read, write and organise your e-mail messages. Beneath the toolbar is a drop-down list of <u>folders</u> (page 100). The main area has two panes:

● The messages pane lists the headers of the messages in the current folder.

● The bottom pane is where messages are displayed – just click on one in the list to pull it into this pane.

Take note

The Preview Pane can be the bottom or right half of the Window, or removed altogether. If it is turned off, a new window will open to display a message when you click on it.

These three copy the message into the New Message window for editing and sending on

Send messages and get new mail

Create new message   Reply   Reply to all   Forward   Delete

Folder list

Header

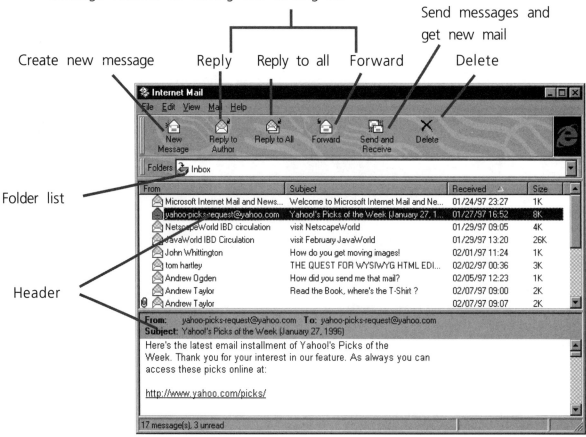

Basic steps

Display options

❑ **Selecting header items**

1 Open the **View** menu, and select **Columns**.

2 Select an item from the **Available** list and click **Add >>** to include.

3 Select an item from the **Displayed** list and click **<< Remove** to remove.

4 Adjust the positions the **Move** buttons.

❑ **The Preview Pane**

5 Open the **View** menu, select **Options** then pick your **Split**.

You can choose which items from the headers to include in the message lists, and how to split the screen.

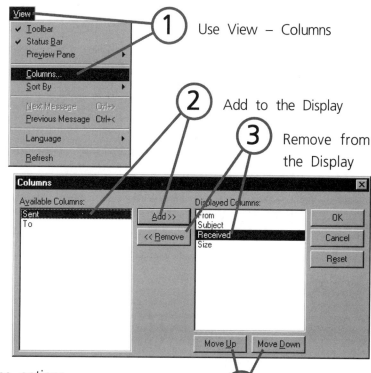

Use View – Columns

Add to the Display

Remove from the Display

Adjust positions

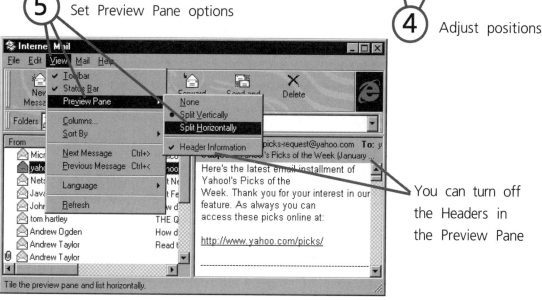

Set Preview Pane options

You can turn off the Headers in the Preview Pane

Mail options

These options are entirely that – optional! The only crucial options are on the Server panel, and they will have been set up by the Wizard (page 86). These pages cover some of the key options that you should consider.

● Don't touch the settings on the Server or Connection panels unless you change your provider, or have trouble getting through.

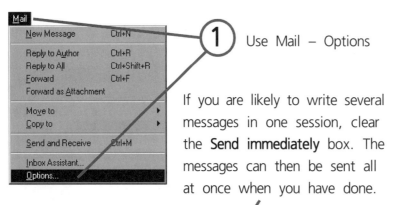

Use Mail – Options

If you are likely to write several messages in one session, clear the **Send immediately** box. The messages can then be sent all at once when you have done.

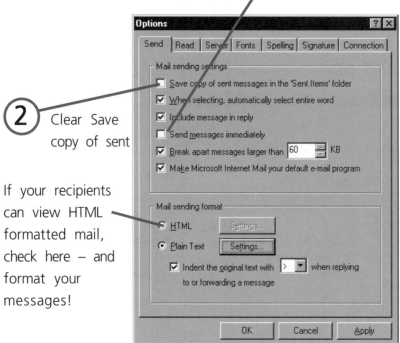

② Clear Save copy of sent

If your recipients can view HTML formatted mail, check here – and format your messages!

1 Open the **Mail** menu and select **Options...**

2 On **Send**, only check **Save copy of sent** ... if you really need copies.

3 On **Read**, clear the **Check for new...** box, unless you have very long sessions on-line.

4 Tick **Empty messages from Delete...** – it will save you a chore.

5 On **Spelling**, turn on all the **Ignore** options.

6 On **Signature**, If you want a Signature (page 103), type it, or link to the file, then select where to add it.

Tip

You may prefer to leave these alone until you have been using the mail long enough to get a clear idea of how you want to work.

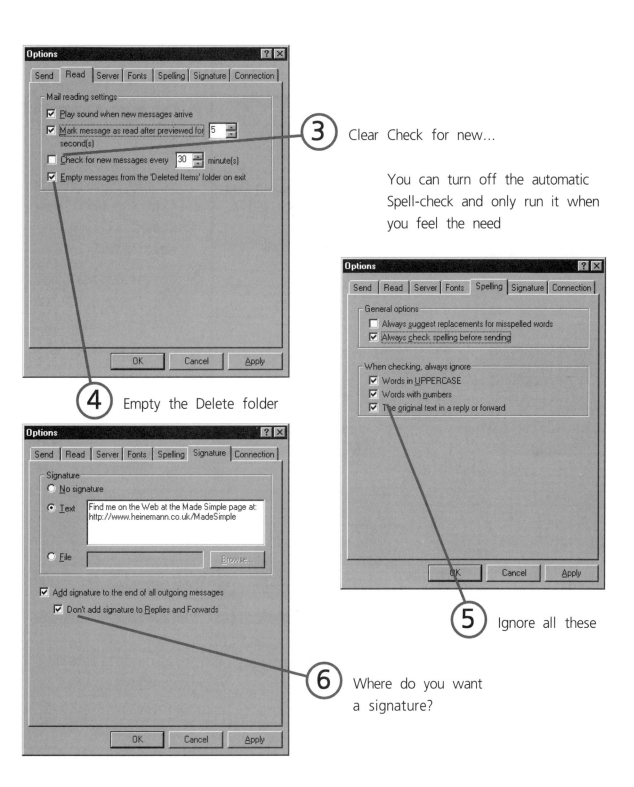

Options ? ✕

Send | Read | Server | Fonts | Spelling | Signature | Connection |

Mail reading settings
☑ Play sound when new messages arrive
☑ Mark message as read after previewed for 5 ⬍ second(s)
☐ Check for new messages every 30 ⬍ minute(s)
☑ Empty messages from the 'Deleted Items' folder on exit

OK | Cancel | Apply

③ Clear Check for new…

You can turn off the automatic Spell-check and only run it when you feel the need

④ Empty the Delete folder

Options ? ✕

Send | Read | Server | Fonts | Spelling | Signature | Connection |

General options
☐ Always suggest replacements for misspelled words
☑ Always check spelling before sending

When checking, always ignore
☑ Words in UPPERCASE
☑ Words with numbers
☑ The original text in a reply or forward

OK | Cancel | Apply

⑤ Ignore all these

Options ? ✕

Send | Read | Server | Fonts | Spelling | Signature | Connection |

Signature
○ No signature
⦿ Text   Find me on the Web at the Made Simple page at:
         http://www.heinemann.co.uk/MadeSimple

○ File   [   ] Browse…

☑ Add signature to the end of all outgoing messages
   ☑ Don't add signature to Replies and Forwards

OK | Cancel | Apply

⑥ Where do you want a signature?

91

E-mail addresses

If you are going to write to other people, you must have their e-mail address – and if you are going to write to them often, you should keep the address in your Address Book.

There are two ways to get an address into your book:

● Write it into the book at any time, on- or off-line.

● The easy way – start to reply to the person and let the system extract the address from the To: entry.

Basic steps

☐ **The Address Book**

1 Open the **File** menu and select **Address Book…**

2 At the **Address Book** window, open the **File** menu and select **New Contact**, or click the **New Contact** button.

3 On the **Personal** panel type the person's name and e-mail address.

4 Click **Add**.

or

        cont…

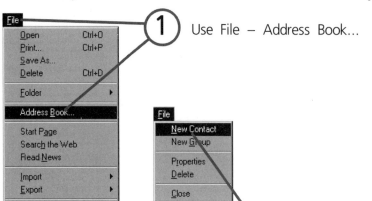

Use File – Address Book…

Set up a New Contact

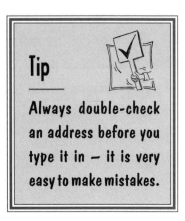

Tip

Always double-check an address before you type it in – it is very easy to make mistakes.

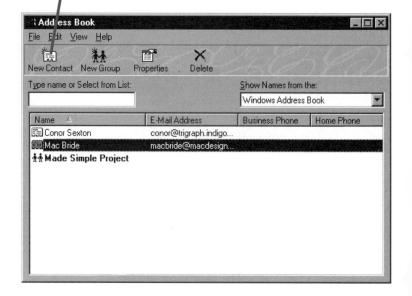

5 Go to the other panels to add further details.

6 Click **OK**.

You don't have to include both First and Last names

The address is transferred to here. If there are several, add them all then set one as the Default.

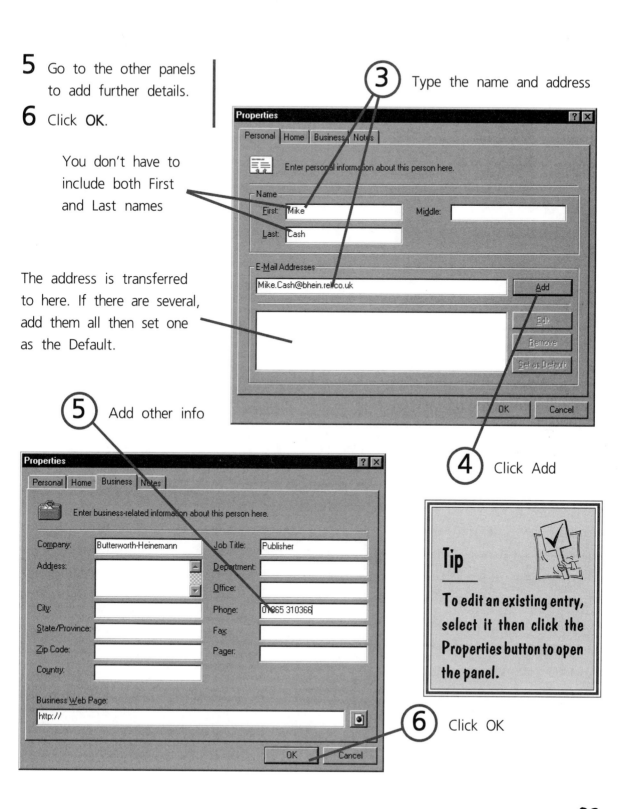

③ Type the name and address

Properties ? X

Personal | Home | Business | Notes |

Enter personal information about this person here.

Name
First: Mike   Middle:
Last: Cash

E-Mail Addresses
Mike.Cash@bhein.rel co.uk   Add

Edit
Remove
Set as Default

OK   Cancel

④ Click Add

⑤ Add other info

Properties ? X

Personal | Home | Business | Notes |

Enter business-related information about this person here.

Company: Butterworth-Heinemann   Job Title: Publisher
Address: Department:
                                    Office:
City: Phone: 01865 310366
State/Province: Fax:
Zip Code: Pager:
Country:

Business Web Page:
http://

OK   Cancel

Tip

To edit an existing entry, select it then click the Properties button to open the panel.

⑥ Click OK

93

Capturing an address

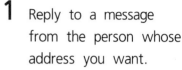

You can copy an address from the *To:* slot of a <u>New message</u> (page 96), into the Address Book. This is not the best way to create a new entry if you are typing it in yourself, but can be a neat way to capture an address from someone who has written to you.

① Start to reply

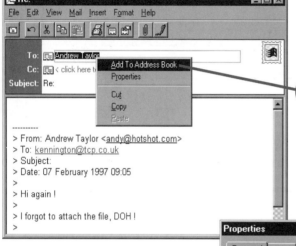

② Select Add To Address Book

> From: Andrew Taylor <andy@hotshot.com>
> To: kennington@tcp.co.uk
> Subject:
> Date: 07 February 1997 09:05
>
> Hi again !
>
> I forgot to attach the file, DOH !
>

1 Reply to a message from the person whose address you want.

2 Right click on the To: entry to open the short menu and select **Add To Address Book**.

3 Edit the names if necessary.

4 Click **OK**.

③ Edit if necessary

④ Click OK

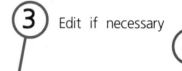

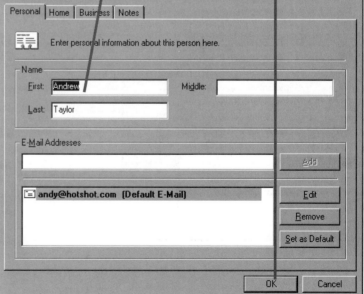

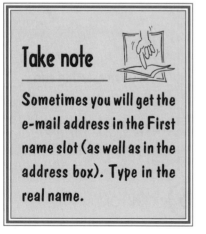

Take note

Sometimes you will get the e-mail address in the First name slot (as well as in the address box). Type in the real name.

Basic steps

Mail groups

1 In the **Address Book** click **New Group**.

2 Type in a **Group Name**.

3 Click **Add**.

4 At the **Select Group Members** dialog box, select a name from the list and click **Add->**.

5 Repeat step 4 for each member.

6 Click **OK** to close **Select**, then again at the **Properties** box.

If you regularly send messages to the same set of people, you can create a mail group. One message composed to the group will then be sent to all.

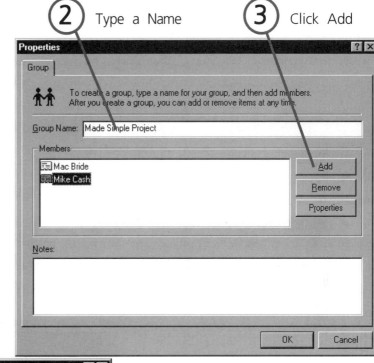

② Type a Name   ③ Click Add

④ Add each person

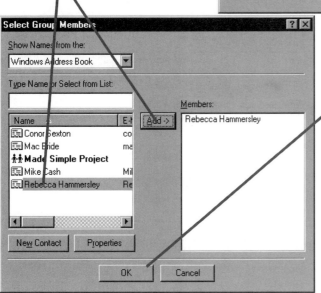

⑥ Click OK

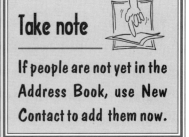

Take note

If people are not yet in the **Address Book**, use **New Contact** to add them now.

Sending messages

To send e-mail, all you need is the address – and something to say! Messages can be composed and sent immediately if you are on-line, or composed off-line and stored for sending later.

Basic steps

1 Open the **File** menu in the *Browser* or the **Mail** menu in the *Mail* window and select **New Message…**

2 Type the **To:** address.

or

3 Click **To:** to open the **Select Recipients** panel.

4 Select the names and click the **To->** or **Cc->** buttons to copy them to the **recipients** lists.

5 Click **OK**.

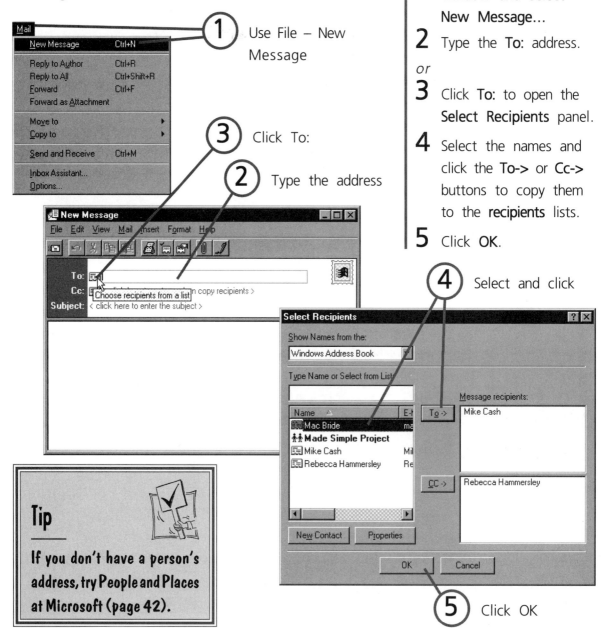

① Use File – New Message

③ Click To:

② Type the address

④ Select and click

⑤ Click OK

Tip

If you don't have a person's address, try People and Places at Microsoft (page 42).

96

6 Type a Subject.

7 Type your message.

8 If you are using HTML, select text and format it as required.

9 Click 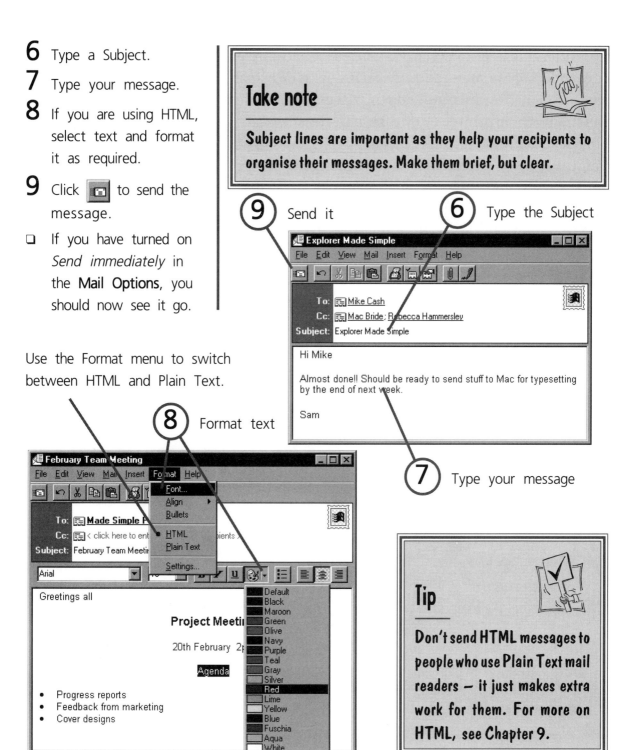 to send the message.

❑ If you have turned on *Send immediately* in the **Mail Options**, you should now see it go.

Use the Format menu to switch between HTML and Plain Text.

Take note

Subject lines are important as they help your recipients to organise their messages. Make them brief, but clear.

⑨ Send it

⑥ Type the Subject

Explorer Made Simple

File Edit View Mail Insert Format Help

To: Mike Cash
Cc: Mac Bride; Rebecca Hammersley
Subject: Explorer Made Simple

Hi Mike

Almost done!! Should be ready to send stuff to Mac for typesetting by the end of next week.

Sam

⑧ Format text

⑦ Type your message

February Team Meeting

File Edit View Mail Insert Format Help

To: Made Simple P
Cc: < click here to ent   ients >
Subject: February Team Meetin

Font...
Align
Bullets
HTML
Plain Text
Settings...

Arial

Greetings all

Project Meetin

20th February 2

Agenda

- Progress reports
- Feedback from marketing
- Cover designs

Default
Black
Maroon
Green
Olive
Navy
Purple
Teal
Gray
Silver
Red
Lime
Yellow
Blue
Fuschia
Aqua
White

Tip

Don't send HTML messages to people who use Plain Text mail readers — it just makes extra work for them. For more on HTML, see Chapter 9.

Files by mail

Files of any type – graphics, word-processor and spread-sheet documents, audio and video clips – and URL links, can be attached to messages and sent by e-mail. Compared to sending them printed or on disk in the post, e-mail is almost always quicker, often more reliable and – up to a point – cheaper. The larger the file, the longer it takes to get through, and the greater the chance of errors – increasing transmission time even more. Somewhere over 1Mb, depending upon the time and cost of postage, the time you and your recipient spend on-line will start to outweight the postage costs.

If you can type a URL into a message at any time, but if you are on a page and want to send its URL to someone, there is a File option that will do the donkey work for you.

1 Compose the message as normal.

2 Open the **Insert** menu and select **File Attachment**

3 Browse through your folders and locate the file.

4 Click **Attach**.

❑ The file will be shown in a panel at the bottom of your message.

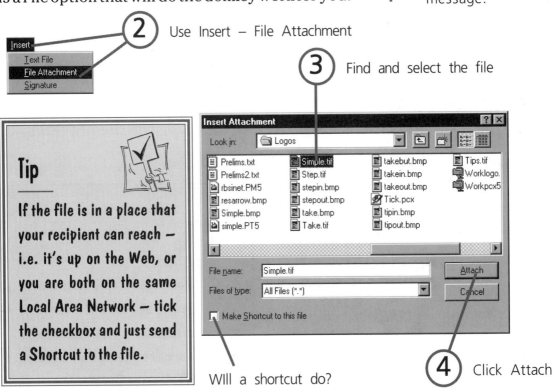

② Use Insert – File Attachment

③ Find and select the file

Tip

If the file is in a place that your recipient can reach – i.e. it's up on the Web, or you are both on the same Local Area Network – tick the checkbox and just send a Shortcut to the file.

Will a shortcut do?

④ Click Attach

❑ **To attach a URL**

6 Go to the page.

7 Open the **File** menu, point at **Send To**, then select **Mail Recipient**.

or

8 Click the **Mail** button, and select **Send a Link**.

9 The URL will be in the Subject line and also present as a Link in the bottom panel. Enter your recipient and a message.

Use Mail – Send a Link

If you decide not to send the file, select and delete the icon

⑦ Use File – Send To – Mail Recipient

⑨ Add the recipient and your message

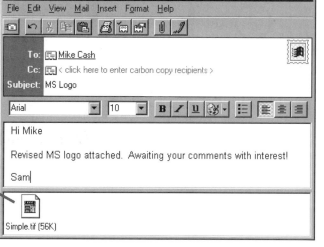

Tip

If you receive an attached file in your mail, treat it as you would a _file in the news_ (page 115).

99

Mail folders

There are initially four mail folders:

Inbox   where new mail arrives
Outbox   for messages awaiting delivery
Sent   for copies of outgoing mail
Deleted   where messages are stored after deletion from other folders. These will be removed at the end of the session if you have set the Empty messages from Delete... option (page 90).

If you keep some of your messages for future use, set up one or more new folders for long-term storage. You might have one for each project, topic or set of contacts – at the very least, you should have an *Old Mail* folder so that your Inbox doesn't get too cluttered.

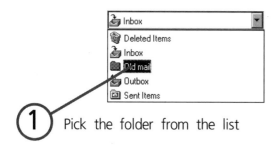

Pick the folder from the list

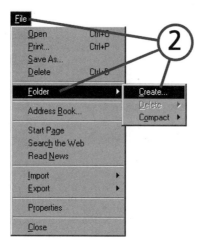

Use File – Folder – Create

❑ **Opening folders**

1 Drop down the Folders list and click on the one you want to open.

❑ **Creating a new folder**

2 In the Mail window, open the File menu, point to Folder and select Create...

3 Give it a name.

❑ **Moving and copying**

4 Select the message to be moved (or copied).

5 Right click on it to open the short menu.

6 Point to **Move to** (or **Copy**) then select the target folder.

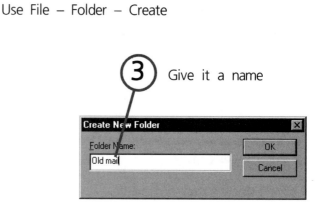

Give it a name

100

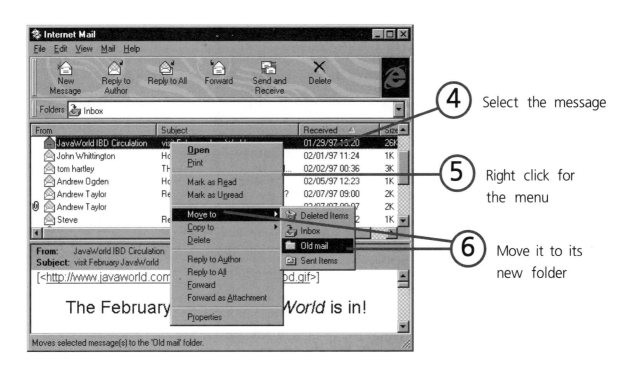

④ Select the message

⑤ Right click for the menu

⑥ Move it to its new folder

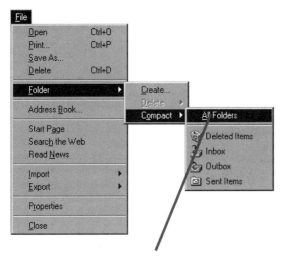

You may as well select All Folders and do a thorough job!

Take note

If you get a lot of mail, and tend to keep messages for future reference, they could take up quite a bit of space after a while. From time to time, use the Folder – Compact command. Messages will still be accessible – they are just stored more efficiently. You should also go through your old mail now and then and delete stuff that is no longer relevant.

E-mail etiquette

When you send someone a paper letter, you know that what they receive will be the same as you send, and if you enclose lots of material, you will pay the extra postage.

E-mail is different. Your recipients actively download your messages, which takes time and can cost money. Further, if they are using any other software than Explorer, it can affect the appearance – and sometimes the *delivery* – of your messages.

Text and data files

A lot of business users, and some individuals, have e-mail systems that can only handle plain text. If you want to send files to these people, the files must first be converted to text. That is easy for you – just set the option when attaching the file. However, there are several formats for sending data files as text, and your recipient must have a suitable converter to extract the file at the other end.

Size

Some e-mail systems set a limit to the size of messages. 1000 lines (roughly 60Kb) is a typical maximum. You are hardly likely to write this much, but an attached file can easily push the message size over the limit.

Even where there is no limit, file size is still a factor. The larger the file, the longer it takes to download, and the higher your recipients' phone bills – especially if they are paying long-distance charges to their providers. With a good modem and a standard phone line, e-mail usually comes in at under 1Kb per second, or 1Mb in 20 minutes.

Use the standard WinZip (or PKZip) software to compress data files before attaching them. Graphics and documents

E-tiquette rules

- ❏ **Small is beautiful.** Short messages are quick and cheap to download.

- ❏ **Test first.** When sending anything other than plain text, try a short test file first to make sure that the other person can receive it properly.

- ❏ **Zip it up!** If you are sending files, compress them with WinZip.

- ❏ **Subject matters!** Always type a Subject line so that the other person can identify the message.

- ❏ **Short signatures.** If you have a signature, keep it short – no more than half a dozen lines. Long files, no matter how clever, are an irritating waste of space.

files can be reduced to 10% or less of their original size this way. Even executable files – the most difficult to compress – show some reduction.

Subject lines

A clear Subject line identifies a message. Your recipients need this when the mail arrives, to see which to deal with first – and which to ignore completely! They also need it when organising old mail, so that they know which to delete and which to place in what folder.

Signatures

A signature file can be added to the end of every message. This is a plain text file, usually saved as *personal.sig* or something similar, containing your name, e-mail address and any other contact details you want to give. People's signatures often also contain a favourite quote, advert, or a picture or name created from ASCII characters. e.g.

Example 1

```
-------------
Sam Kennington        |kennington@tcp.co.uk

Computing's Made Simple at http://www.heinemann.co.uk/bhsimple/simple.html
-------------
```

Example 2

```
------------------------
Gary
```

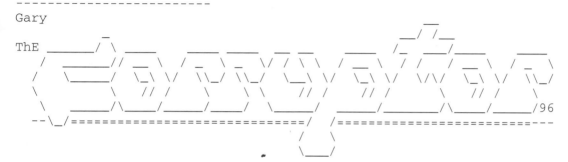

Summary

- The **Mail Wizard** will take you through the process of setting up your mail system.

- The **Mail window** is divided into two panes, for the headers and message text. Folders are selected from a drop-down list.

- The easiest way to handle e-mail addresses is to store them in your **Address Book**.

- **Addresses can be picked up** from the To: slot as you are sending or replying to mail by the system, or you can type them in yourself.

- When **sending messages**, start by selecting who they will go to. You should always write the nature of the message in the Subject line.

- **New mail folders** can be created to store old mail. Messages can be easily moved between folders.

- **Deleting a message** from a folder moves it to the Delete folder. Delete it from here to get rid of it altogether.

- **E-mail etiquette** is based on not wasting other people's time (and phone bills). Mail should be kept short, and should have a clear Subject line.

- **Signatures** can add something extra to your mail — and long ones can add far too much!

8 The News

Newsgroups

These have developed from e-mail, but instead of articles being mailed directly to you, they are sent in bulk to your news server, and you download them from there.

At the last count there were over 20,000 groups, each dedicated to a different interest – professions and obsessions, programming languages and TV programmes, hobbies, politics, sports, fan clubs and all the rest.

- The quality and volume of the articles vary enormously. Some newsgroups circulate large quantities of interesting and relevant articles; some carry few articles, and even they are hardly worth reading.

- Some newsgroups are moderated, i.e. they have someone who checks all incoming articles before broadcasting them to the members. This reduces the quantity of irrelevant and/or boring post.

- Some groups are mainly for discussions, others are more like open help-lines, where people can ask for – and get – solutions to technical problems.

- Not all newsgroups are available on all servers.

- As newsgroups bring together people who share a common interest, they can be a good place to make new friends.

- Subscribing to a group simply allows you to download its articles from your server. Subscription is free of charge, and you can join – or leave – a group at any time.

- You can read the articles in any newsgroup without actually subscribing.

The main sections

Usenet

comp	Computing
news	Newsgroups
rec	Recreational
sci	Scientific
soc	Social and cultural
talk	Debate-oriented

Other

alt	all kinds of topics
biz	business
gnu	Unix systems
uk	UK-based

... and more...

Take note

Most newsgroups are part of USENET – the Users Network – a loose collection of individuals and organisations. Other old networks brought their own groups into the Internet as well.

Newsgroup names

Tip

If you are new to the Internet, there is a group specially for you. It's *news.announce.newusers.* (For subscribing see page 111.)

Newsgroups are organised into a branching structure, with major sections sub-divided by topic. Their names reflect this structure.

For example, **comp.lang.basic.visual.database** is in the **comp**uter section, which amongst other things covers programming **lang**uages, including **basic**, and this has a **visual** subsection containing four groups, one of which is concerned with **database** programming.

You can see the full list of the newsgroups availabe on your server, by opening this dialog box. Using keywords, you can focus on particular types of groups, when you want to select one to <u>subscribe</u> or <u>sample</u> (page 111), but one day – when you have a spare hour or two – work through the whole list just to see what's there.

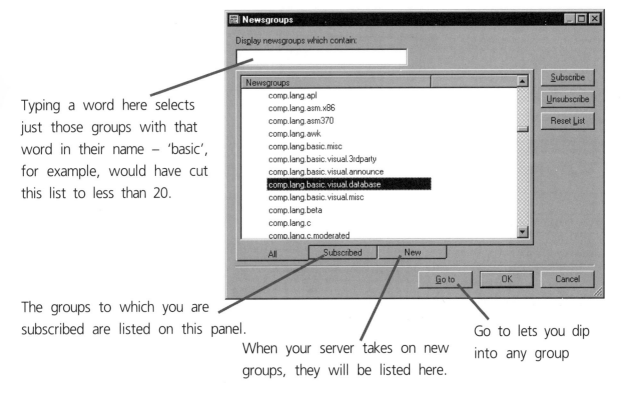

Typing a word here selects just those groups with that word in their name – 'basic', for example, would have cut this list to less than 20.

The groups to which you are subscribed are listed on this panel.

When your server takes on new groups, they will be listed here.

Go to lets you dip into any group

The News Wizard

The first time that you try to read the news, a Wizard will run to collect the necessary details and set things up for you. As always with wizards, you just need to follow the instructions – but before you start, make sure that you have this information at hand:

● your e-mail address

● the name of your service provider's news server.

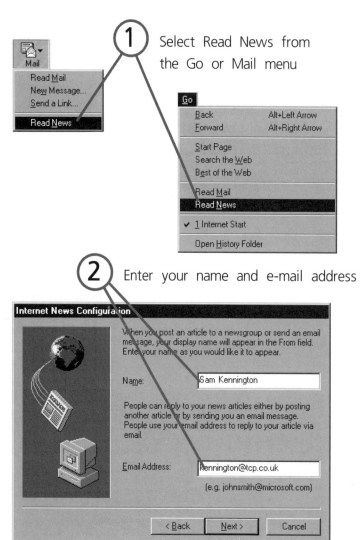

① Select Read News from the Go or Mail menu

② Enter your name and e-mail address

1 In the Explorer window, click **Mail** and select **Read News** or use **Go – Read News**.

❏ The first time you do this, the News Wizard will run. Work through its dialogs, clicking **Next** after each.

2 Enter your real name and e-mail address – these will be added to any articles you post.

3 Type in the name of your news server.

4 Select your connection method – most of us Use a modem...

5 If you have more than one dial-up connection, select the one to your news server.

6 Click Finish and wait. Explorer will connect and download the list from the server – it takes a while!

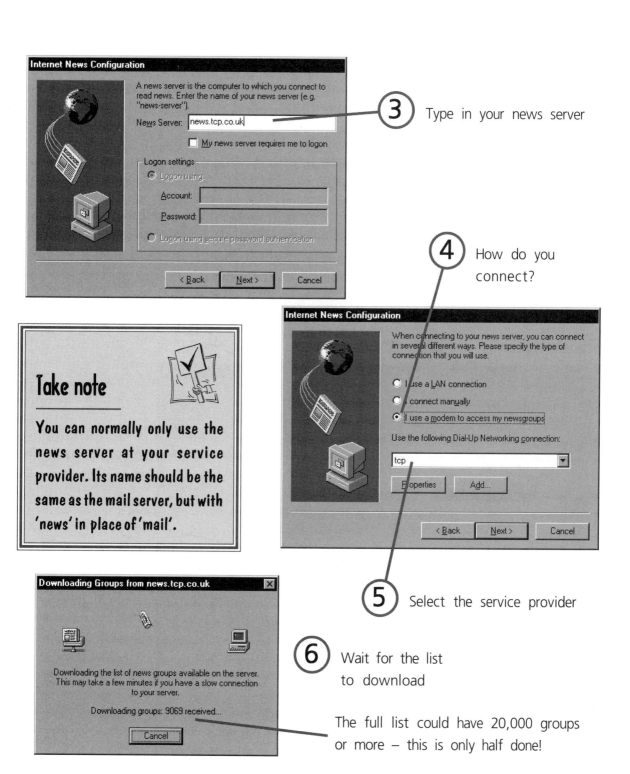

Internet News Configuration

A news server is the computer to which you connect to read news. Enter the name of your news server (e.g. "news-server").

News Server: news.tcp.co.uk

☐ My news server requires me to logon

Logon settings

◉ Logon using:

Account:

Password:

○ Logon using secure password authentication

< Back | Next > | Cancel

(3) Type in your news server

(4) How do you connect?

Internet News Configuration

When connecting to your news server, you can connect in several different ways. Please specify the type of connection that you will use.

○ I use a LAN connection

○ I connect manually

◉ I use a modem to access my newsgroups

Use the following Dial-Up Networking connection:

tcp

Properties | Add...

< Back | Next > | Cancel

Take note

You can normally only use the news server at your service provider. Its name should be the same as the mail server, but with 'news' in place of 'mail'.

(5) Select the service provider

Downloading Groups from news.tcp.co.uk

Downloading the list of news groups available on the server. This may take a few minutes if you have a slow connection to your server.

Downloading groups: 9069 received...

Cancel

(6) Wait for the list to download

The full list could have 20,000 groups or more – this is only half done!

The News window

Access to newsgroups is handled through the News window. This looks very like the Mail window, and is used in much the same way.

The top pane holds the headers of the current articles in the selected group; the lower pane will display the text of an article when it is selected.

The drop-down list of newsgroups has those groups to which you have subscribed, plus folders posted and saved articles, and the group that you last dipped into. Select one from here and – if you are on-line – the system will download the headers for that group.

❏ **Reading the news**

1 Open the **Newsgroups** list and select a group.

2 Select an article and wait a moment for it to be downloaded into the lower pane.

① Select from the Newsgroups list

③ Click Newsgroups

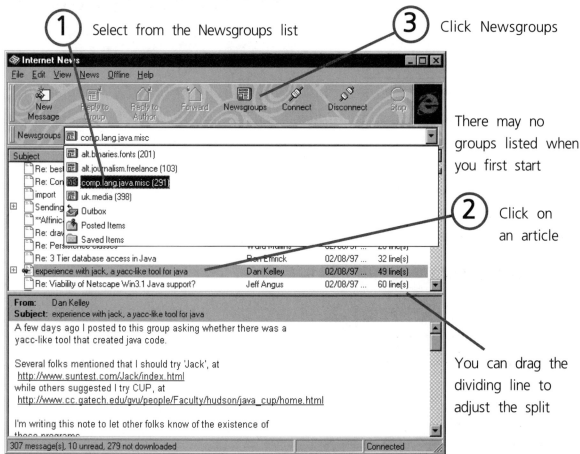

There may no groups listed when you first start

② Click on an article

You can drag the dividing line to adjust the split

Sampling and subscribing

3 From the **News** menu, select **Newsgroups...** or click the **Newsgroups** button.

4 Open the **All** groups panel.

5 Type a word to filter the list.

6 Select a group.

7 See what's there by clicking **Go to**

or

8 Join the group by clicking **Subscribe**.

If you want to dip into other groups, or see what's available so that you can subscribe to some, open the newsgroups panel. Rather than struggle with the full list, filter it with a word that is likely to be in the name.

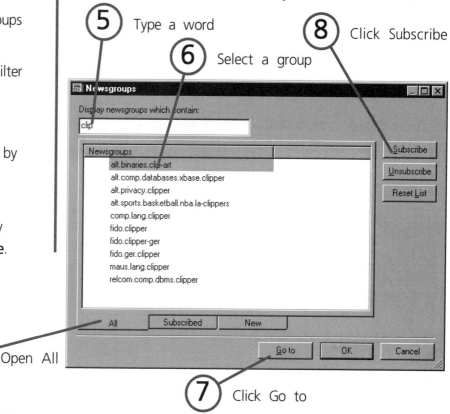

⑤ Type a word

⑥ Select a group

⑧ Click Subscribe

④ Open All

⑦ Click Go to

Take note

Your news server may not carry all newsgroups. Some don't carry those that circulate graphics and other binary files as the volume of data adds heavily to the traffic on their lines; some filter out those that may carry pornographic material. Censorship and self-censorship are subject to lively debate on the Internet. If you want to follow this further, the main **UK** discussion site is at:

    http://www.leeds.ac.uk/law/pgs/yaman/yaman.htm

Posting and replying

Posting articles to a newsgroup is very similar to sending mail, but with a couple of significant differences:

● when posting to a newsgroup, your message goes to thousands of people – observing the <u>netiquette</u> (page 114) is very important.

● when responding to an article, you have the choice of replying to the author only, to the whole group or to both at once.

If your message is *truly* relevant to several groups, you can write other group names in the Cc: slot

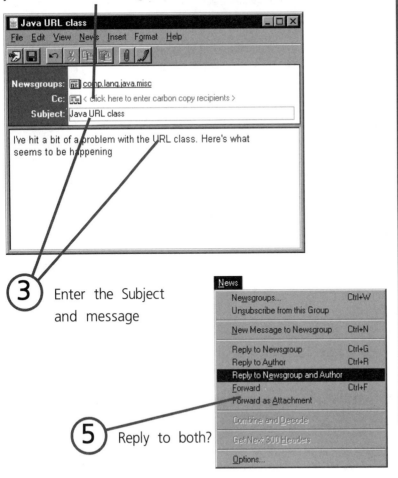

③ Enter the Subject and message

⑤ Reply to both?

Basic steps

❏ **Posting articles**

1 Open the **Newsgroups** drop-down list and select the one in which you want to post.

2 Click the **New Message** button or use **News – New Message**.

3 The group's name will be in the **To:** slot. Enter the **Subject**, and type your message.

❏ **Responding to articles**

4 Select the article.

5 Use the News option to Reply to Newsgroup and Author

or

6 Use the buttons to reply to the Author only or to the whole group.

7 Edit unwanted lines from the quoted article.

8 Type your reply.

9 Click the **Send** button.

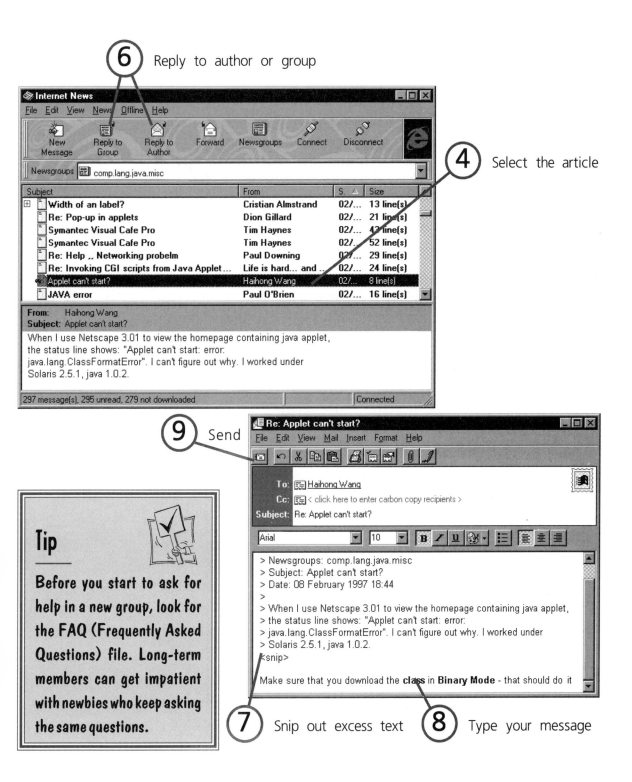

6 Reply to author or group

4 Select the article

9 Send

Tip

Before you start to ask for help in a new group, look for the FAQ (Frequently Asked Questions) file. Long-term members can get impatient with newbies who keep asking the same questions.

7 Snip out excess text

8 Type your message

113

Newsgroup netiquette

The rules are mainly aimed at not wasting other people's time (and connection charges!), but there is also a large element of trying to encourage a fruitful and co-operative atmosphere within the groups.

- DO write a very clear Subject entry so that others will know what the article is about.

- DO keep articles brief and to the point.

- DO trim unnecessary lines out of quotes when posting replies to articles.

- DO 'lurk' (read without posting) for a while before you start to post. That way you will learn the range and nature of topics that are covered by the group.

- DO read the FAQs (Frequently Asked Questions) lists before you start to post questions to a group. The answers may already be there.

- DON'T post 'off-topic'. Articles must be relevant to the newsgroups.

- DO be tolerant of others – they may be young, inexperienced or struggling with English as a foreign language.

- DON'T overreact – abusive articles do not contribute anything useful to discussions. If you do feel strongly about something someone has written, step back, calm yourself and write a reasoned response. And if that provokes an angry reply, let it drop.

- DO make it clear when you are joking, as not everyone will share your sense of humour. They can't see that you are smiling, so add a <grin> or a Smiley :-).

Tip

The worst breach of Netiquette is to start a 'flame war'. A message attacking or abusing other people or their beliefs will almost certainly lead to a spate of angry articles in response. Though the matter may be important to those of you engaged in the row, it will probably be a waste of space for all the other readers in the newsgroup.

Basic steps

1 Check the Subject line. If it says (1/1) at the end, it is a simple one-part file, and you can carry on.

2 Open the article.

3 Click the Paperclip icon to display the filename.

4 Click the filename to open the file.

5 Some files generate a warning message – only open the file if you feel it is safe.

The file will be opened either in Explorer or in a <u>viewer</u> (page 14).

❑ **Saving attached files**

6 Right click for the short menu and select the **Save** option.

7 Select the folder in which to store it.

8 Type in a **Filename** *with the correct extension.*

9 Click **Save.**

Files in the News

A key feature of the news (and e-mail) system is that it is based on 7-bit transfers. That is, the bytes coming down the wires only use 7 bits for data, with the eighth bit being using for error-checking. This is fine for plain text, as this only uses the first half of the ASCII set (characters 0 to 127) and these can be represented with only 7 bits.

Graphics, zipped files, executable programs and similar files – known as binaries – present a problem, as you have to use all 8 bits to express the values in these. To transfer a binary file through the mail or news systems, it must be converted to 7-bit format for transfer and converted back to 8-bit before it can be used.

To make matters worse, some systems set a limit to the size of articles and messages (around 60Kb). Large binary files have to be split into smaller chunks before transfer.

Most of the time you won't have to think about any of this, as Explorer can happily cope with the two most commonly used encoding formats, MIME and uuencode. A couple of mouse clicks should be all that is needed to view or save the file. The only problems you are likely to have are with <u>multi-part files</u> (page 118).

The filename is usually in the Subject line

(1) Is it a single-part file?

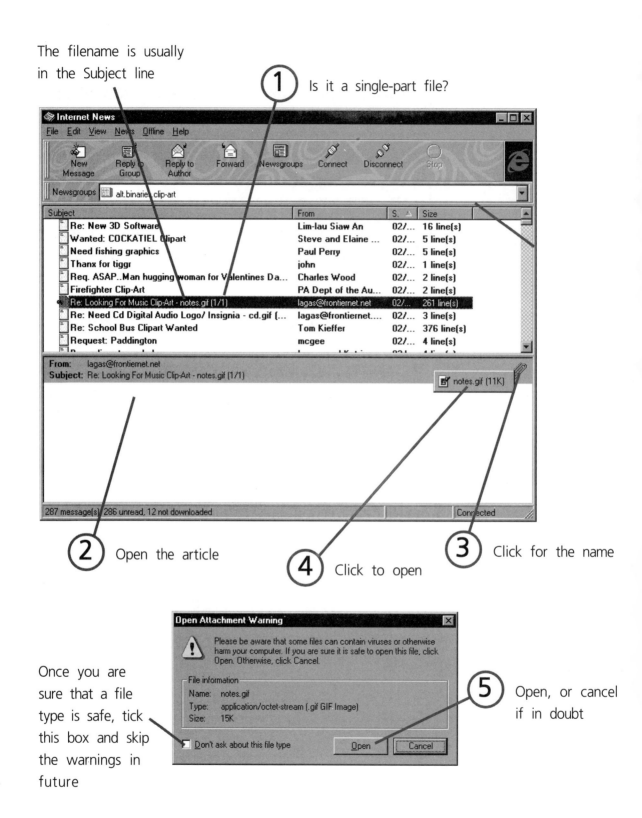

(2) Open the article

(4) Click to open

(3) Click for the name

Once you are sure that a file type is safe, tick this box and skip the warnings in future

(5) Open, or cancel if in doubt

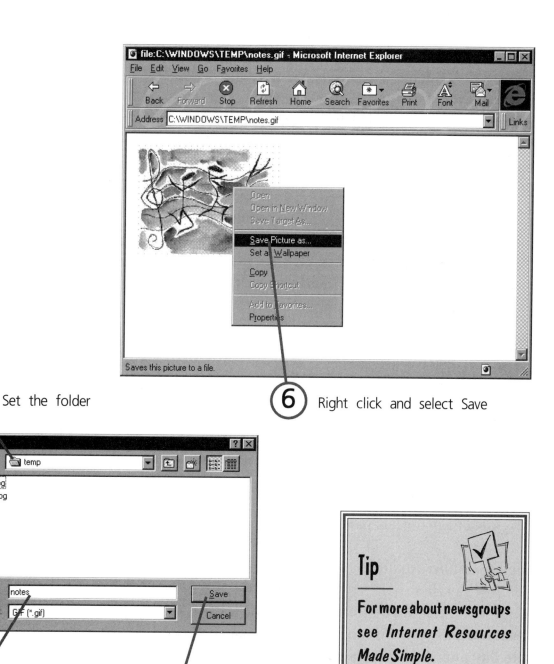

⑦ Set the folder

⑥ Right click and select Save

⑧ Enter a filename

⑨ Click Save

Tip

For more about newsgroups see *Internet Resources Made Simple.*

Multi-part files

These can be recognised by the numbers at the end of the Subject. (1/1) identifies a simple one-part file; (2/4) tells you this is the second part of a 4-part file. Split files are a problem. Only the first will be viewable, and will show only part of the image. If you want the whole file, you must save all the related articles, join them together and decode them.

The two most commonly used coding formats are *MIME* and *uuencode*. Systems that use MIME (Multipurpose Internet Mail Extension) can usually cope with large files, so these are very rarely split. Multi-part files are far more likely to be uuencoded.

Uuencoding

This was designed for Unix to Unix transfers (hence UU) – much of the Internet runs on Unix systems – but it is widely used as it is simple and efficient.

Uuencoded files always start:

    begin 644   (or 600, or 777 – the numbers vary)
followed by the name of the binary file.

The last line of the last part of the code is marked by:

    end
Multi-part files usually have breaks marked by:

    - - - cut here - - -
To decode uuencoded files use Windows UUCoder (*wuudo486.exe*). You can find this at most shareware sites, including the Windows specialist:

    www.winsite.com

1 Open each article and use **File – Save** to save it as a text file.

2 Edit each file, deleting everything down to the 'begin', after the 'end', and the 'cut here' lines. Save the files.

3 Use WordPad or other word processor to copy and paste the separate files into one. Save the combined file.

4 Run **wuudo486**.

5 Select **File – Decode**.

6 Find the file to be decoded.

7 At the Save As dialog, change the folder or filename if desired. That's it!

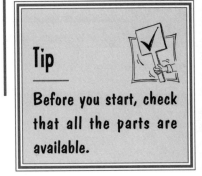

Tip

Before you start, check that all the parts are available.

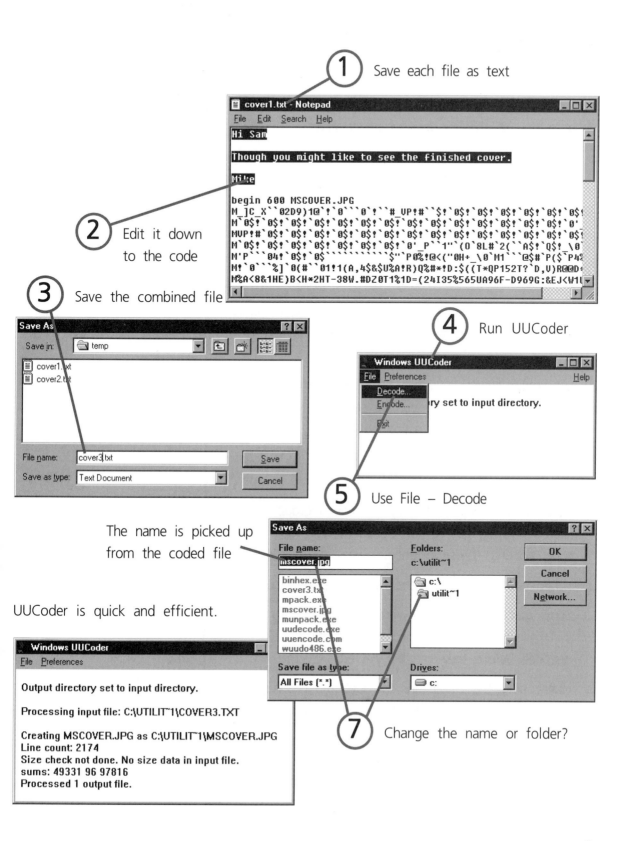

① Save each file as text

cover1.txt - Notepad

File Edit Search Help

Hi Sam

Though you might like to see the finished cover.

Mike

begin 600 MSCOVER.JPG
M_]C_X``02D9)1@`!`0```0``#`#``#``
M`0$
MUP
M
M'P
M
M%A'HE

② Edit it down
to the code

③ Save the combined file

Save As

Save in: temp

cover1.txt
cover2.txt

File name: cover3.txt   Save

Save as type: Text Document   Cancel

④ Run UUCoder

Windows UUCoder

File Preferences   Help

Decode...
Encode...   ry set to input directory.
Exit

⑤ Use File – Decode

The name is picked up
from the coded file

Save As

File name: Folders: OK
mscover.jpg   c:\utilit~1
                                       Cancel
binhex.exe   c:\
cover3.txt   utilit~1   Network...
mpack.exe
mscover.jpg
munpack.exe
uudecode.exe
uuencode.com
wuudo486.exe

Save file as type: Drives:
All Files (*.*)   c:

UUCoder is quick and efficient.

Windows UUCoder

File Preferences

Output directory set to input directory.

Processing input file: C:\UTILIT~1\COVER3.TXT

Creating MSCOVER.JPG as C:\UTILIT~1\MSCOVER.JPG
Line count: 2174
Size check not done. No size data in input file.
sums: 49331 96 97816
Processed 1 output file.

⑦ Change the name or folder?

Summary

- Run the **News Wizard** to take you through the process of setting up the link to your news server.

- There is a **newsgroup** for almost every conceivable interest, hobby, profession or obsession.

- Newsgroups are **organised into a hierarchy**, branching down from broad areas to highly specialised topics.

- The first stage in using any News system is to **download the list of newsgroups** from your server.

- Explorer's **News** window, like the Mail window, is divided into two panes, for the headers and text of articles.

- **Subscribed** newsgroups can be selected from the drop-down list, but any can be **sampled** from the full list in the Newsgroups dialog box.

- When **responding to an article**, you can post a follow-up article to the group, reply to the author, or both.

- You can **post articles** to any subscribed group. Articles should only be posted to relevant newsgroups. Off-topic postings cause offence.

- When posting, observe the newsgroup **netiquette**.

- Some **graphics** can be viewed and saved easily. Others will have been encoded into text and must be decoded before they can be viewed.

- **Uuencoding** and **MIME** are the two most common formats for transmitting binaries through newsgroups.

- **Large files** may be spread over several parts and must be reassembled in a word-processor before they can be decoded.

9 HTML

Internet Assistant

HTML – HyperText Markup Language – is the system used to produce Web pages. Essentially, it is a set of tags that specify text styles, draw lines, display images, handle URL links and the other features that create Web pages. You can create HTML documents in NotePad or Word, but a decent HTML editor offers a quicker and easier way to make a Web page. Internet Assistant adds HTML editing facilities to Word, making it able to handle most – though not all – aspects of HTML.

If you have Word, download Internet Assistant (free) from Microsoft. At 1.3Mb, it should download in less than 15 minutes. Installation is far quicker!

1 Go to Microsoft's Start Using page and select Internet Assistant, or head directly to: **www.microsoft.com/msword/internet/ia**

2 Download the file (**wdia204z.exe** or something similar) into a temporary directory.

3 Run the file from Windows Explorer.

4 The Setup program offers only one option. Click **Change Folder** if you prefer to organise your own storage.

5 Click **Launch Word** at the end.

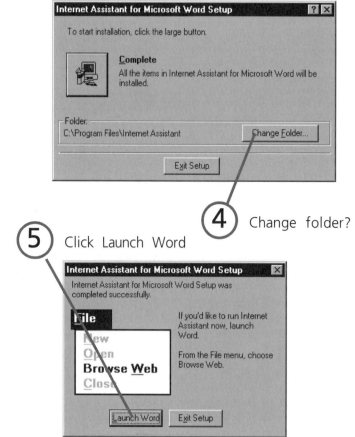

④ Change folder?

⑤ Click Launch Word

Tip

Internet Assistant is also available to work with Excel, Access and PowerPoint.

122

Web Browse view

Tip

The main point of using HTML is to create your Home page on the Web. If your access provider does not offer Web space, switch to one that does!

When you launch Word, with Internet Assistant, for the first time, it will open an introductory page. Some useful tips can be picked up from here, but before you start clicking on the links, look for a moment at what has happened to Word.

There is a new toolbar, carrying *browsing* tools – Word now has a Web Browse viewing mode. There is also a second toolbar, for the new HTML <u>Edit view</u> (page 125) and we will get to that shortly.

History list

Open URL

Open and add to a
Favorites list in Word

Home (opens the page shown here)

Stop

Reload

Switch to Edit View

Back

Forward

Cilckable link

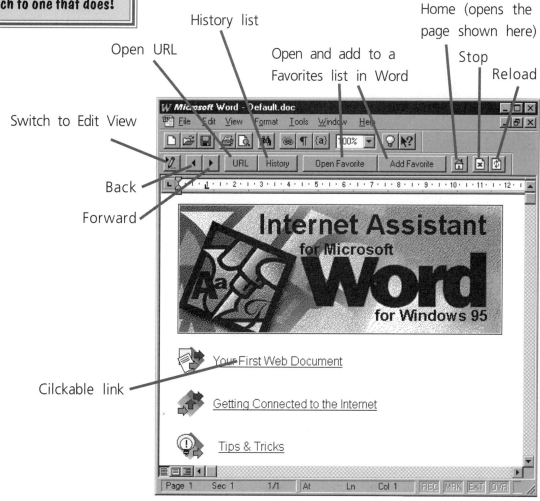

Starting a new page

All Word documents are based on a template, which defines the basic layout and the selection of text styles. If you want to create a Web page, you must use the HTML template. To get that you must either set it as the default – not a very good idea if you use Word more for other purposes – or start from the New dialog box.

Use File – New

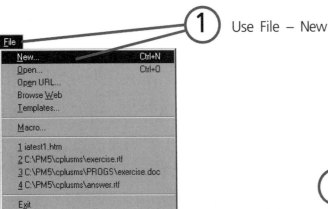

Select the HTML template

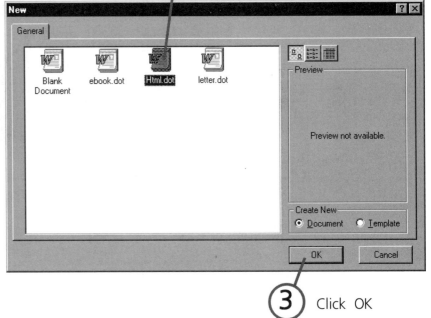

Click OK

Basic steps

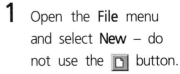

1 Open the **File** menu and select **New** – do not use the 🗋 button.

2 At the **New** dialog box, select the template **Html.dot**.

3 Click **OK**.

❏ The document will open with the HTML Edit View toolbar at the top of the window.

Tip

If you want to know more about using Word, have a look at *Word Made Simple,* in this series.

The HTML Edit View toolbar

Tip

Use the Styles as a first step in formatting text, then tweak the display with bold, italics, font size and other tools.

Some of these buttons are standard Word formatting tools; some are present in Explorer; others are specific to Internet Assistant – chiefly those used to insert images, links and lines into the text.

The menus have also acquired a few extra items, most of which we will look at in the next few pages.

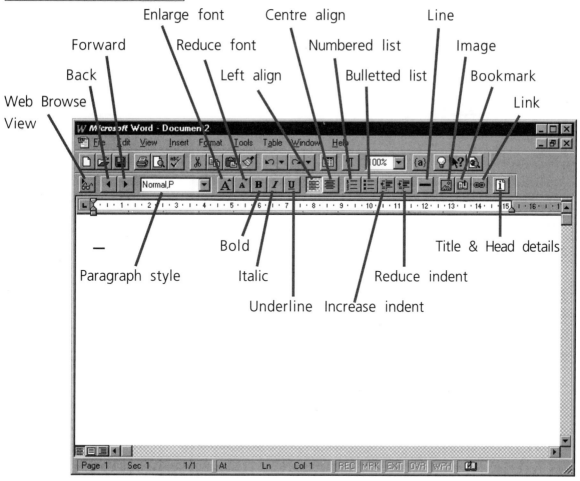

Enlarge font
Forward
Reduce font
Centre align
Numbered list
Line
Image
Back
Left align
Bulletted list
Bookmark
Web Browse View
Link

Paragraph style
Bold
Italic
Underline
Increase indent
Reduce indent
Title & Head details

Formatting text

The simplest way to format text is to use the drop-down list of Paragraph Styles. These include:

- six levels of Headings, from 24 point down to 9 point – smaller than Normal text;

- Bulletted or Numbered Lists – and you can create lists inside lists where several levels are needed;

- Pre-Formatted, which retains a layout created with spaces and tabs – all the other styles squeeze out excess spaces;

- Address, by convention used to format your e-mail address at the bottom of your home page;

- Normal – the default.

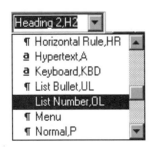

Take note

When other users view your page, they may not see the same display that you do – it depends on the browser they are using, and any font and size settings that they may have made on their system.

Tags

When you click on a tool to apply a format to some text, the editor writes HTML tags into the document for you. These are keywords, written inside <angle brackets> and are usually in pairs – at the start and the end of the formatted text. To see the HTML tags, use **View – HTML Source**.

Look at the page and source opposite and try to relate the tags to the displayed text.

The text at the top of the Source, between the <HEAD> tags, is for information only – it is not displayed on screen. (See page 140.)

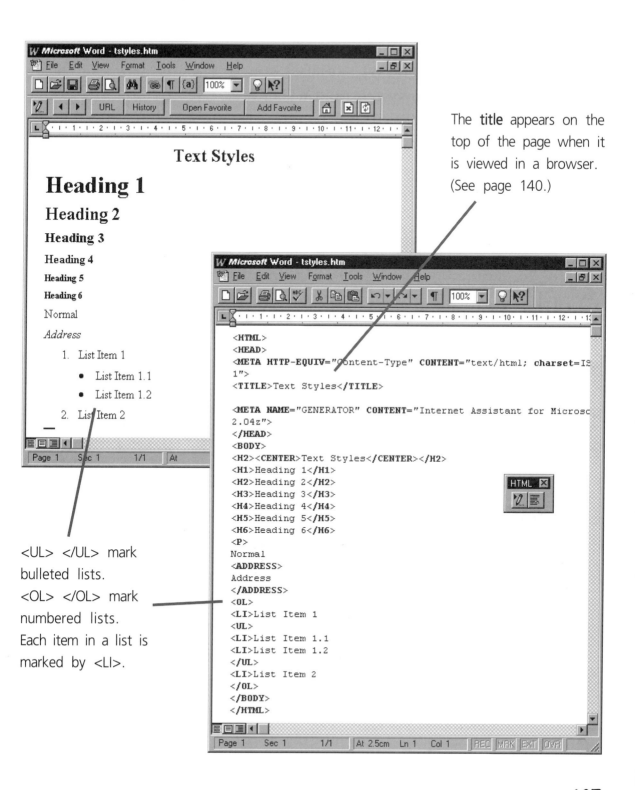

The **title** appears on the top of the page when it is viewed in a browser. (See page 140.)

<UL> </UL> mark bulleted lists.
<OL> </OL> mark numbered lists.
Each item in a list is marked by <LI>.

Links

Without links there would be no Web, so spin a few of your own! There are essentially three types of links:

- to other pages on your system (and in your Web space, once they're uploaded)
- to pages or files at remote sites
- to another part of the same page.

The first two types of link are created in the same way. For links within a page, you must create a *bookmark*–a place that can be linked to. (In standard HTML these are called *anchors*.)

Basic steps

- ☐ **Links off the page**
- **1** Select the words (or image) that will hold the link.
- **2** Select **Insert – HyperLink** or click 🔗
- **3** Click **Browse** and locate the local page.

or

- **4** Type the URL of the remote page or file.
- **5** Click **OK**.

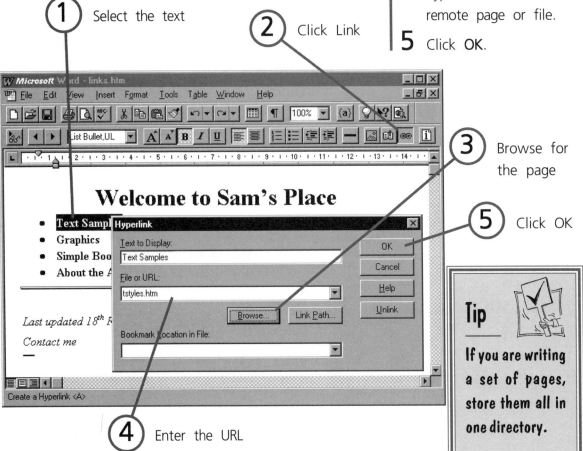

① Select the text

② Click Link

③ Browse for the page

⑤ Click OK

④ Enter the URL

Tip

If you are writing a set of pages, store them all in one directory.

Basic steps

- ❏ **Links within the page**

1 Place the cursor where you want a bookmark.

2 Select **Edit – Bookmark** or click 📖

3 Give the bookmark a name.

4 Click **Add**.

5 Move to where you want to link from, select the words and click 🔗

6 Select the bookmark from the **Location in File** list.

7 Click **OK**.

You cannot use spaces in a name – under_lines are acceptable

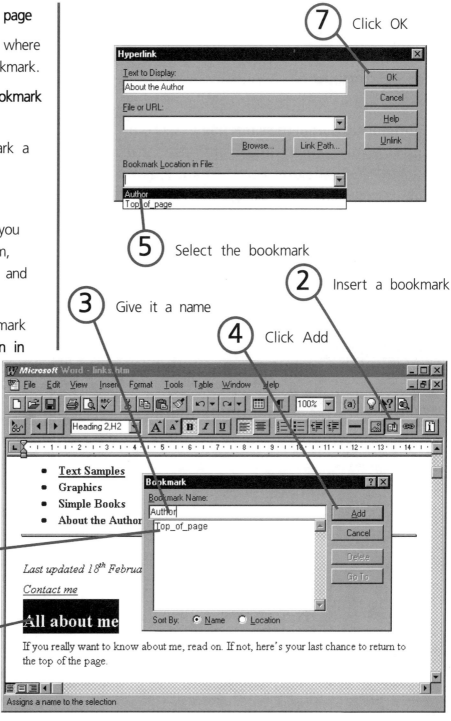

⑦ Click OK

⑤ Select the bookmark

③ Give it a name

② Insert a bookmark

④ Click Add

① Go to the jump point

Pictures

Pictures add a lot to Web pages – in two ways. They add to the appearance, making pages more attractive and interesting, but they also add to the download time. If you are going to include pictures, they should be no larger than is necessary to do the job.

The format of the images is important. Use only the GIF and JPG formats. They have built-in compression, producing small files, and can be handled directly by almost all browsers. Bitmapped (.BMP) images – the sort produced by Paint or Paintbrush – have relatively large files and should not be used.

With 'transparent' GIFs, the page's background shows through unpainted parts of the image

Basic steps

1 Place the cursor where you want the image.

2 Select **Insert – Picture** or click 🖼

3 Type the filename or click **Browse**.

4 At the **Insert Picture** dialog, select the file.

5 Type **Alternative Text**, for readers who don't want to or cannot view images.

6 Click **OK**.

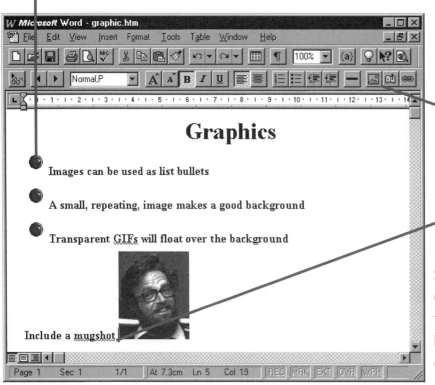

② Click Insert Picture

① Position the cursor

Some large images cannot be displayed – to see these, use the Preview in Browser command (page 132)

Alternative Text

There are some users who access the Web through systems that can't display images, and many that choose to turn off images, for faster browsing. Write something in the Alternative Text so that they know what they are missing.

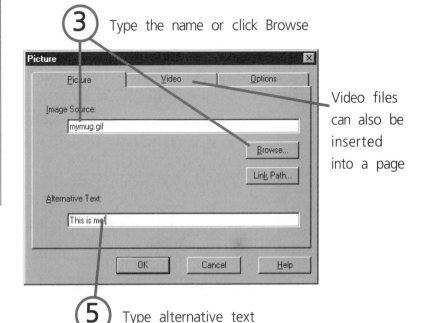

③ Type the name or click Browse

Video files can also be inserted into a page

⑤ Type alternative text

④ Select the file

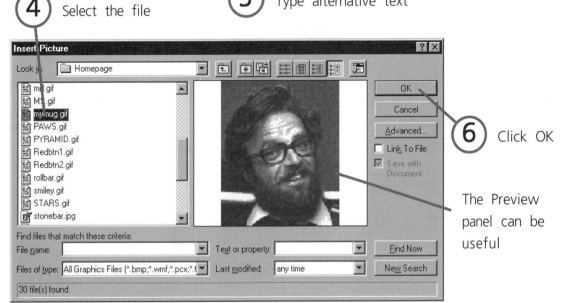

⑥ Click OK

The Preview panel can be useful

Backgrounds

If you want a background picture, use a small one that can be repeated, tile-fashion, to fill the page. These are added through the Background and Links panel.

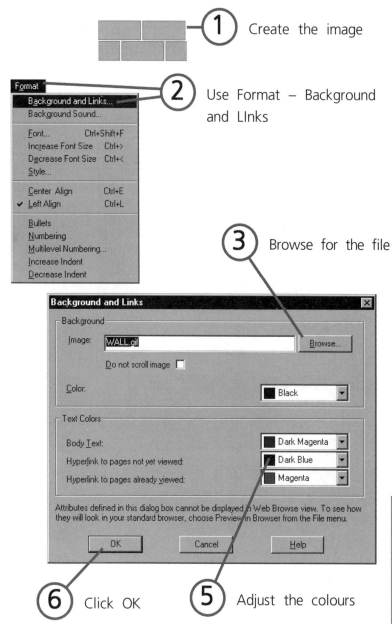

Create the image

Use Format – Background and Links

Browse for the file

Click OK

Adjust the colours

Basic steps

1 Create a small GIF or JPG image in a graphics program.

2 Open the **Format** menu and select **Background and Links**.

3 Click **Browse**.

4 At the **Insert Picture** dialog, select the file.

5 If necessary, change the text colours to suit the background.

6 Click **OK**.

❑ Background pictures are not displayed by Word – all you see is the <BODY...> tag that shows the background has been set.

7 Save the file.

8 Use **File – Preview in Browser** to see the effect.

Take note

Preview in Browser is only available from Edit View.

132

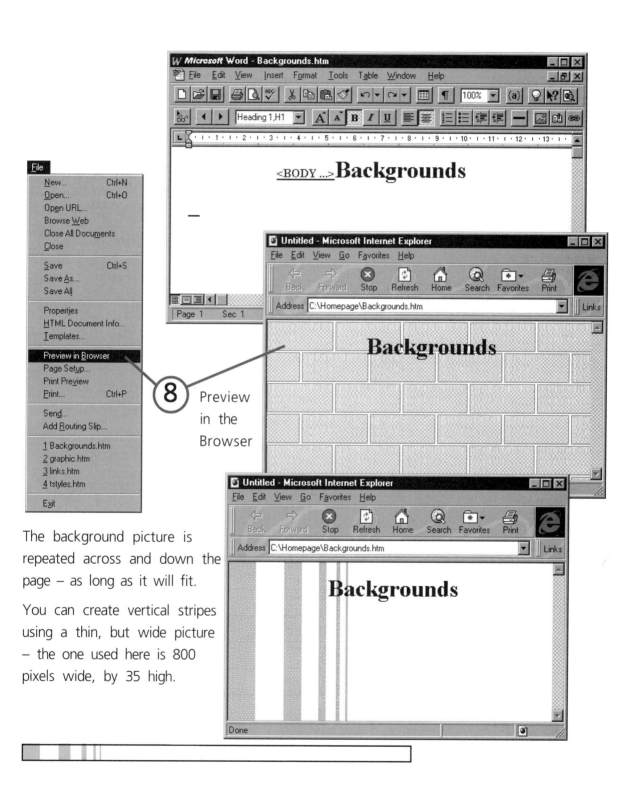

The background picture is repeated across and down the page – as long as it will fit.

You can create vertical stripes using a thin, but wide picture – the one used here is 800 pixels wide, by 35 high.

Tables

Tables are very fiddly things to construct if you write the code directly – look at the HTML Source after you have made a table! Internet Assistant makes things easy.

Before you start, sketch out the table on paper – it saves having to adjust it later.

```
Made Simple Books    Out Now    1997
Applications            22        8
Internet                 5        4
Programming              0        8
```

This needs a table of 4 Rows and 3 Columns. Initially, all the text will have the Normal style. Once it is typed in, the top row and left column text can be restyled as Headings.

Basic steps

1 Use **Table – Insert Table** or click ▦.

2 Set the number of **Rows** and **Columns**.

3 Click **OK** to create the blank table.

4 Enter text into the cells, using [Tab] to move from one to the next.

5 Select the cell(s) and format the text using the toolbar.

6 From the **Table** menu, **select Border** and set the width and colour.

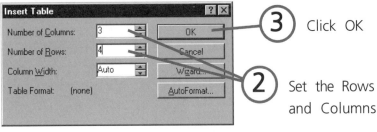

③ Click OK

② Set the Rows and Columns

④ Enter text

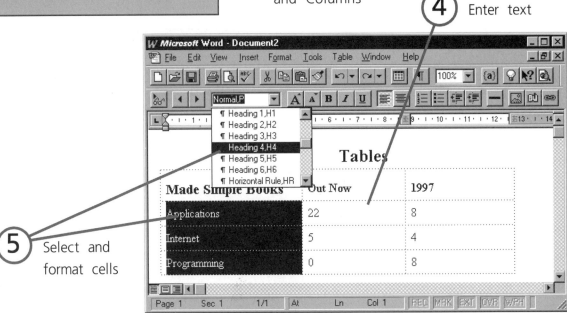

⑤ Select and format cells

7 Use other **Table** options to fine tune the display.

8 Word does not display tables accurately – use **Preview in Browser** to check the appearance.

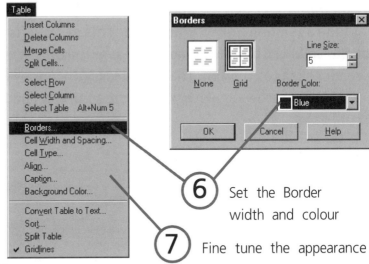

⑥ Set the Border width and colour

⑦ Fine tune the appearance

The table can be aligned at the left or centre of the page.

Text can be aligned across the width of cells (as normal) and *vertically* within them.

⑧ Preview in the Browser

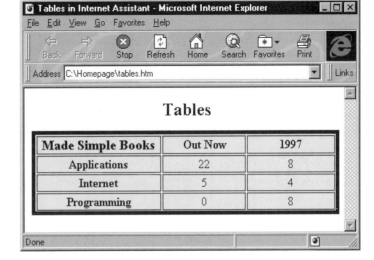

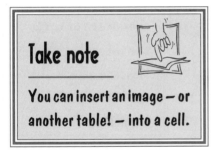

Take note

You can insert an image – or another table! – into a cell.

Feedback

If you want readers to be able to get in touch with you, include a mailing link in your page. This should have *mailto:* followed by your e-mail address as the URL. When a reader clicks on this link, the New Message window will open in their browser, with your address already in the Mail To slot.

1 Type in suitable text, such as *Mail to me* and select all or part of it.

2 Click 🔗

3 Enter *mailto:* followed by your e-mail address.

4 Click **OK**.

① Select the link text

② Click Insert Link

④ Click OK

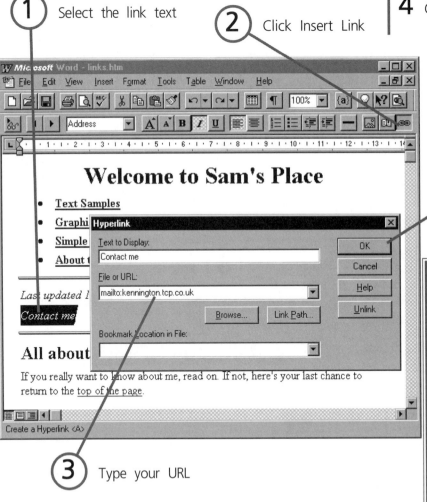

③ Type your URL

Tip

To test the mailto link, preview the page in the browser and click on the link. You should get a New Message window with your e-mail address in the Mail To slot.

136

Forms

The simple example given on the next two pages shows some of the main features of forms and their construction.

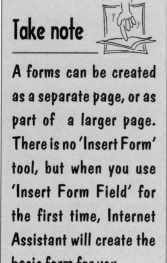

Take note

A forms can be created as a separate page, or as part of a larger page. There is no 'Insert Form' tool, but when you use 'Insert Form Field' for the first time, Internet Assistant will create the basic form for you.

Forms are an excellent way to get feedback from your visitors – or at least, from those who are browsing with Netscape. It is an unfortunate fact that Explorer does not manage forms well. When browsing with Explorer you can fill in a form, but the Submit button simply starts a New Message window for you to write to the form's owner!

The simple example given on the next two pages shows some of the main features of forms and their construction. It has three types of *fields*, for collecting data, plus a little accompanying text. You might like to follow the steps to create a copy, then adapt and extend it to fit your needs.

Text field

Plain text and images can be added as needed.

Radio buttons – visitors can only select one of these.

If you want to get the right feedback, you've got to ask the right questions!

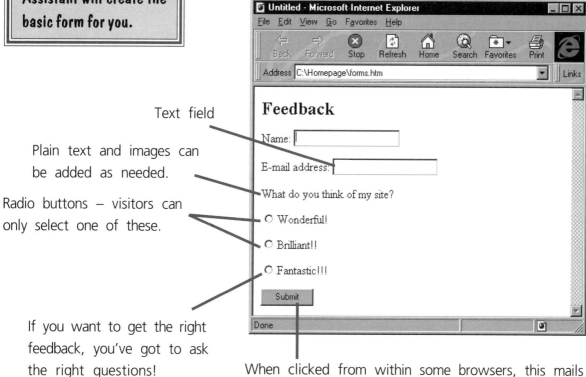

When clicked from within some browsers, this mails the form's data to you. Clicking in Explorer starts up a New Message window, with your address, so that visitors can write to you.

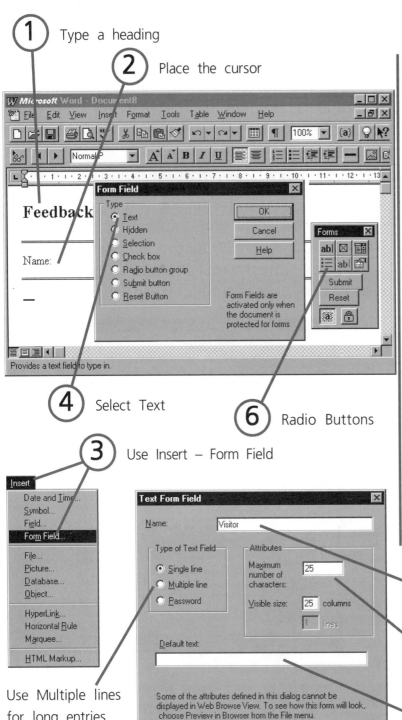

① Type a heading

② Place the cursor

④ Select Text

③ Use Insert – Form Field

⑥ Radio Buttons

⑤ Give it a name

Use Multiple lines for long entries

How big a slot do you need?

Sometimes you will want to suggest an answer

1 Type any heading text.

2 Place the cursor where you want a field.

3 Use **Insert – Form Field** to create the first field.

4 Select the **Text** type.

5 Give the field a **Name** and set options.

6 Type a question and click :☰ to create a **Radio Button** group.

7 Type each button name and **Add** it to the group, then click **OK**.

8 Click ⬚Submit to create a **Submit** button.

9 Give it a **Name**, then set up a mailto: link as the **Action**, and select POST as the **Method**.

⑦ Give a name and add buttons

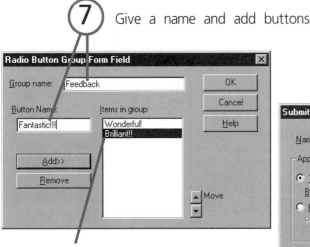

The Button names appear
as their captions on screen.

⑨ Give a name and set up the action

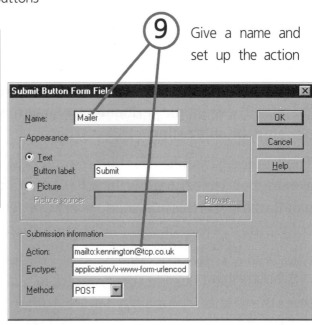

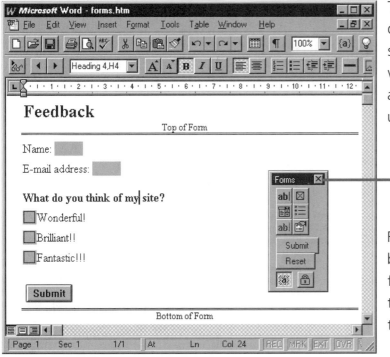

The Action is normally mailto: done by a POST. With some service providers this may not work. If you have problems, ask your provider how to set up a form on their server.

Close the toolbox when you have finished.

Fields are shown as grey blocks in Word. To see the form properly – and to test the Submit button – preview the page in your browser.

Finishing touches

Headers and keywords

The <HEAD> area is invisible unless you view the document source, but it is important. This is the part that holds the page's title, its author's name, and the keywords that search engines will use for classifying – and for finding – the page. These should be done for any page that you want people to be able to find.

The Title is easily done – it is just a matter of writing it into a dialog box. Unfortunately, Internet Assistant does not handle the rest of this information very well. The simplest solution is to write the details directly into the code.

Each item is written in a <META...> tag. This has two parts – the NAME identifies what the type of data, and CONTENT gives the details. The main types are *Author*, *KeyWords* and *Classification*.

<META...> tags are ignored by browsers, but search engines do look for them. Those that use KeyWords or Classification, will pick up the META tag NAME and use the CONTENT for indexing the page.

Basic steps

1 From the File menu select HTML Document Info.. or click **[i]**.

2 Enter the Title.

3 Click OK.

4 From the View menu select HTML Source.

5 Type the META tags into the HEAD area.

6 Return to Edit View.

These should indicate what's on the page. Give as much as you like, separating the words or phrases by commas.

```
<HEAD>
    <TITLE>Text styles</TITLE>
    <META NAME="Author" CONTENT="Sam Kennington">
    <META NAME="KeyWords" CONTENT="HTML, text styles, Web pages, World Wide Web">
    <META NAME="Classification" CONTENT="HTML, World Wide Web">
</HEAD>
```

The NAME and CONTENTS text should be enclosed in double quotes.

Tip

There's lots more about HTML in *HTML Made Simple*.

140

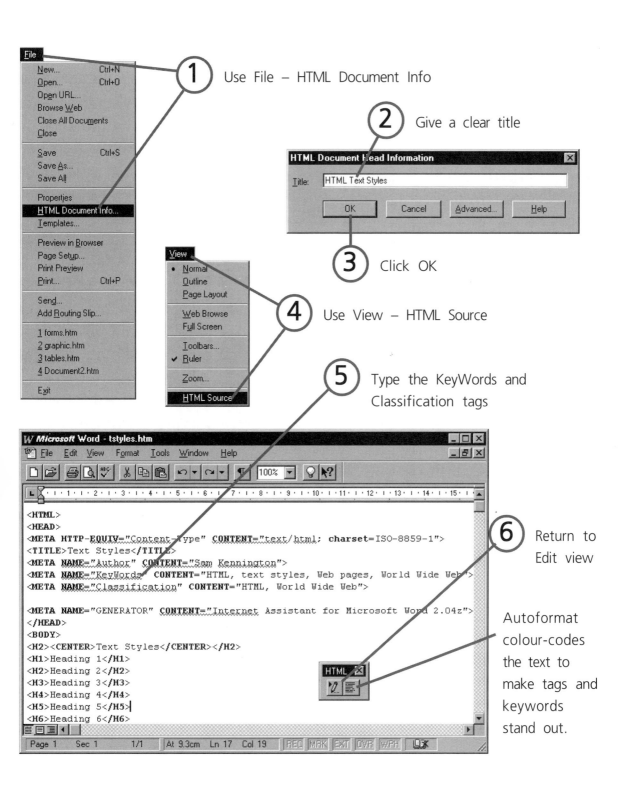

① Use File – HTML Document Info

② Give a clear title

HTML Document Head Information

Title: HTML Text Styles

OK   Cancel   Advanced...   Help

③ Click OK

④ Use View – HTML Source

⑤ Type the KeyWords and Classification tags

⑥ Return to Edit view

Autoformat colour-codes the text to make tags and keywords stand out.

File menu:
- New... Ctrl+N
- Open... Ctrl+O
- Open URL...
- Browse Web
- Close All Documents
- Close
- Save Ctrl+S
- Save As...
- Save All
- Properties
- HTML Document Info...
- Templates...
- Preview in Browser
- Page Setup...
- Print Preview
- Print... Ctrl+P
- Send...
- Add Routing Slip...
- 1 forms.htm
- 2 graphic.htm
- 3 tables.htm
- 4 Document2.htm
- Exit

View menu:
- Normal
- Outline
- Page Layout
- Web Browse
- Full Screen
- Toolbars...
- Ruler
- Zoom...
- HTML Source

Microsoft Word - tstyles.htm

File Edit View Format Tools Window Help

```
<HTML>
<HEAD>
<META HTTP-EQUIV="Content-Type" CONTENT="text/html; charset=ISO-8859-1">
<TITLE>Text Styles</TITLE>
<META NAME="Author" CONTENT="Sam Kennington">
<META NAME="KeyWords" CONTENT="HTML, text styles, Web pages, World Wide Web">
<META NAME="Classification" CONTENT="HTML, World Wide Web">

<META NAME="GENERATOR" CONTENT="Internet Assistant for Microsoft Word 2.04z">
</HEAD>
<BODY>
<H2><CENTER>Text Styles</CENTER></H2>
<H1>Heading 1</H1>
<H2>Heading 2</H2>
<H3>Heading 3</H3>
<H4>Heading 4</H4>
<H5>Heading 5</H5>
<H6>Heading 6</H6>
```

HTML

Page 1   Sec 1   1/1   At 9.3cm Ln 17 Col 19   REC MRK EXT OVR WPH

Publishing your page

To publish your page(s) on the World Wide Web, you must upload all the necessary files to the appropriate place at your access provider's site. Before doing this, check your files, and check your links.

Organising the files

When you upload your files to your access provider's site, they will be copied to one folder, with the links automatically adjusted to match their location. If they are not there already, move the files for your pages and images into one folder – then edit each page containing links and adjust the URLs if necessary.

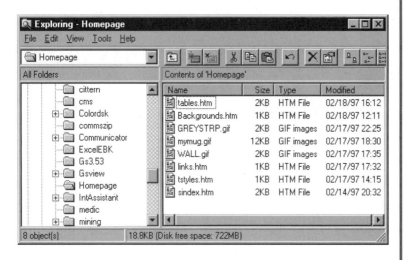

Final testing

Double check the links by loading the home page (the top page of the set) into Internet Explorer. Visit every linked page and make sure that every image is displayed. If you have included links to remote sites, go on-line and check those links.

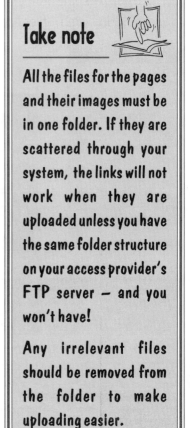

Take note

All the files for the pages and their images must be in one folder. If they are scattered through your system, the links will not work when they are uploaded unless you have the same folder structure on your access provider's FTP server – and you won't have!

Any irrelevant files should be removed from the folder to make uploading easier.

142

Basic steps

Web Publishing Wizard

1 Run **Web Publishing Wizard** from the **Start** menu, in **Accessories – Internet Tools**.

2 **Browse** for the **Folder** with your Web files, to publish the full set.

or

3 **Browse** for a **File** to add or update a page.

4 On the first run, select a service or click **New** and give the details.

5 Follow the Wizard, and wait while it works.

You cannot simply upload your pages from Explorer – it doesn't do file transfers that way round. However, you can download from the Start Using page at Microsoft a (free) Web Publishing Wizard that will do the trick.

The first time you use it, it will need some configuration. If you use CompuServe, AOL or one of the other service providers that the Wizard knows about, configuration will be very simple. In other cases, it may take a little longer and you must supply details of your provider's ftp server and the URL of your home page.

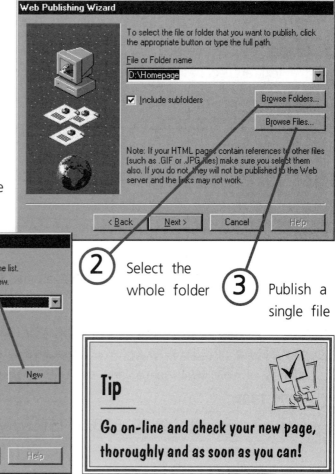

(4) Select a service

Set up a new service if necessary

(2) Select the whole folder

(3) Publish a single file

Tip

Go on-line and check your new page, thoroughly and as soon as you can!

Summary

- **Internet Assistant** makes Web page creation much easier. It can handle text formatting, lines, images, links, tables and forms.

- **Paragraphs can be formatted** to appear as headings, bulletted or numbered lists, or in the *address* style.

- **Selected text** may be made bold, italics or varied in size.

- You can add **links** to your other pages, to pages on remote sites or to a bookmarked point within a page.

- A picture can be set to form a **background**, and will be repeated across and down to fill the window.

- **Pictures** can be inserted anywhere on the page, and the text aligned beside it in several positions.

- **Tables** can be constructed very easily in the editor, but you must use **Preview in the Browser** to see what they really look like.

- To construct a form, Insert **Form Fields** to collect the data, and add any text or pictures as needed.

- If you add **keywords**, search engines will be able to index your site.

- Before uploading your pages, **assemble all the files** into one folder.

- The **Web Publishing Wizard** will transfer your files to your service provider's server. You must give it the **FTP address** of your Web space, and the **URL of your home page**.

- After publishing your page, **check it thoroughly!**

Index